A WORDSWORTH ANTHOLOGY

D0591654

WILLIAM WORDSWORTH

A WORDSWORTH ANTHOLOGY

*A selection from the poems
and Introduction by*

HELEN DAVIES

COLLINS
LONDON AND GLASGOW

COLLINS GREETINGS BOOKLETS

General Editor: G. F. Maine

Printed in Great Britain

COLLINS CLEAR-TYPE PRESS

INTRODUCTION

"I'll kill myself! I swear I will!" A thin resentful child stood with a knife in his hand, trembling with rage at what he considered had been an unjust punishment. He had rushed to lock himself in the attic of his grandfather's house vowing to commit suicide. But presently his angry sobs grew less as he watched the summer clouds moving past the window. He forgot about the knife and soon turned and ran out of the room, through the house, on and on until he reached the edge of the river where he flung himself down panting. His sister, a year younger than he, found him there and crept to his side to console him in her soft little stammering voice. She was relieved to find him enthralled in listening to the music of the running water.

Mrs. Wordsworth worried over her second son. Not many things disturbed her tranquil spirit, but she admitted that of her five children William was the only one about whose future she was anxious, and "he would be remarkable either for good or for evil." What could one make of a child who in a fit of temper took a whip and lashed the canvas of a picture or who was frenziedly excited by the sound of a waterfall? But she was never to see in which direction her passionate little son developed, for she died in 1778 when he was hardly eight years old.

Her husband, stricken with grief, found the older boys too difficult to deal with in addition to his responsibilities as an attorney, and sent Richard and William from Cockermouth to school at Hawkhead. Here was the ideal environment for independent youth hungry for experience. In the unsupervised freedom of after-school hours Wordsworth exulted in the saturation of the senses which contact with the countryside gave him. With boundless energy he walked and climbed, rode and skated, bathed and rowed on the lake. He rejoiced in his feverish quest after new sensation. He read avidly—all Fielding, much Swift, *Gil Blas*, *Don Quixote*. In winter he talked for long hours with his friends in the cottage where he was boarded with old Anne Tyson. He wrote some lines of verse as a school exercise, wrote a few more, and thought of writing much, but he was chiefly occupied in living, in experiencing that close communion with nature which was to provide the "emotion recollected in tranquillity" of his great poetry.

When Wordsworth was thirteen his father died leaving his family in straitened circumstances, for Lord Lonsdale whose agent John Wordsworth was, had "forcibly borrowed" most of the unfortunate attorney's money, and it was not until 1801 that it was repaid, with interest, by Lord Lonsdale's son. Thus it was with difficulty that his guardians found the means to send Wordsworth to Cambridge, but send him they did, and at seventeen this tall, awkward, idealistic youth found himself gazing with eager anticipation at the gothic perfection of King's College Chapel. But although the traditions of the university impressed him, he was disappointed in the superficiality of his fellow students and in the aridity of the lectures. He studied irregularly, allowing himself to be drawn into the frivolities of his companions, always longing for the summer vacation when he could roam the countryside with Dorothy, that fervid spirit for whom her brother was "the building up of my being, the light of my path."

The autumn of 1789 saw Wordsworth an ardent republican. He had spent the summer in France and found her on the eve of the Revolution, "Standing on the top of golden hours." He seized joyfully on the aims of the Revolutionists. Now, like so many other young idealists, he saw in prospect the realisation of his ideals, and more tenaciously than most, he clung to this hope until France in turn became the agressor and his faith expired in bitter disillusionment.

In 1791 Wordsworth took his degree. Academically he had not distinguished himself, but what was much more important for the poet was his spiritual development. His communion with nature had become more complicated and devious. The intrusive "I" with its sophistications now invaded his contact with the world of natural objects, and that former awe-inspiring feeling of one-ness with nature had almost disappeared. Cambridge seemed to leave little impression upon him. He remained singularly unmoved and uninspired by the activities of the university. Yet that indestructible core of independence which caused him to be undisturbed by the world of people around him was also the source of the integrity, the high seriousness of purpose, and the inner joy which are the foundations of his poetry.

In November of this year Wordsworth went to France for the second time, and at Orleans he met and fell in love with a young girl of a Royalist family, Annette Vallon. The following year, after he had been forced to return to England through lack of money, Annette gave birth to his child, and in response to her piteous letters he tried desperately but in vain to reach her on the eve of war. Thus life taught him in the hard school of experience how to resolve the conflict between sensualism and asceticism, enriched his emotional awareness and enlarged his insight into human character. The reflection of this experience is found to underlie, at times subconsciously, many of his poems.

The failure of the Revolution resulted in the collapse of his political ideals. This shock, added to the stress of his personal tragedy, caused Wordsworth to turn in despair to the barren philosophy of Godwinism, and then, wearied by the incessant search for proof, to unhappy scepticism. It was Dorothy who in this crisis brought him solace and inspiration, and under her wise guidance he was able to accept once more the testimony of the heart and the imagination.

In 1795 William and Dorothy were at last able to settle down together after sixteen years of separation. Wordsworth's friend, Raisley Calvert, whom he had nursed to the end of a fatal illness, left them £900, enough to rent "Racedown," a house near the Dorset coast. Here began that friendship with Coleridge which was to prove so fruitful of inspiration and so fraught with anxiety. In the other each found the perfect complement. Coleridge's mecurial genius required guidance and direction, and his personality could fulfil itself only by having one greater than himself to admire; in return he gave Wordsworth the vast resources of his intellect. They visited each other's homes frequently, and went for long tramps over the hills, reciting their verses to one another.

Although the only long poem Wordsworth wrote at Racedown was the gloomy *Borderers* with its cumbersome Gothic literary machinery, nevertheless the certainty of his vocation, which he had first realised at Cambridge, grew daily stronger, and Coleridge's admiration helped to confirm the conviction. Soon after a visit to the Coleridge's cottage in the Quantock Hills the Wordsworths took up residence in Alfoxden, a nearby house, where the two friends planned what was to become a landmark in literature—*The Lyrical Ballads*. Coleridge's contribution, *The Ancient Mariner*, outweighed in poetic value all Wordsworth's put together, with the one exception of *Tintern Abbey*, but Wordsworth never understood the greatness of this masterpiece of the supernatural. In fact he attributed the poor sale of the book to the inclusion of Coleridge's poem! Wordsworth's lack of sound critical judgment of his own and other writer's work, and indeed a certain indifference to the work of others, was a perpetual astonishment to his friends. It was this same lack of discrimination in regard to his own poetry that caused him to inflict on his public so much dull and laborious verse. The drawback of his very sincerity and earnestness was that he considered everything he had to say was worth saying, and was poetry.

The Alfoxden period was one of great productivity. In peaceful surroundings, and congenial and stimulating company, he wrote many short poems, but the era of his great poetry was still to come. While *Tintern Abbey* gave a foretaste, the other verses of the period were often unfortunate illustrations of his theory of realism, which brought out only too strongly that lack of humour which has probably done more harm to Wordsworth's reputation as a poet than anything else. Who can now read *Goody Blake* or *The Idiot Boy* without a smile? This is the Wordsworth who provides the paradise for parodists and the subject of caricature, who provokes quite deserved ridicule. But we must realise that unless he had attacked all subjects with the same seriousness, he would not have been the Wordsworth of the *Prelude* or the *Sonnets* or the *Ode*.

In September, 1798, after the publication of the *Lyrical Ballads*, Wordsworth, Dorothy, Coleridge and a friend, John Chester, went to Germany. After visiting Klopstock, the venerable father of German letters, they separated, and William and Dorothy spent the winter in bitterly cold isolation at Goslar. Having access to few books, and confined indoors by icy weather, the poet turned to composition. Here the limpid "Lucy" poems were written, and the *Prelude* planned. When winter broke up brother and sister wandered over Germany, until early in May they returned to England.

Later that year they settled in Dove Cottage at Grasmere. This was the true beginning of the life of quiet contemplation for which Wordsworth had always longed. But perhaps for Dorothy there now fell a shadow on her perfect happiness as her passion for William grew beyond her understanding, and her love for Coleridge brought her nothing but grief. Dorothy Wordsworth was one who, because of her devotion and gay-spirited sacrifice, deserves to be remembered with gratitude by those who acclaim her brother's genius. Her entire life was spent in ministering to his needs. It was as much for his sake as for her own pleasure that she recorded those observations of nature which in their own way constitute a masterpiece in miniature, and it is possible that her long and final illness of mind and body was caused in part by her too strenuous exertions in accompanying Wordsworth on his long rambles.

At Grasmere a long-standing friendship was consummated, and in October, 1802, Wordsworth married Mary Hutchinson, who had always been Dorothy's dearest friend. Earlier in the year he and Dorothy visited Annette and her daughter, now ten years old, at Calais. There was now no thought of marriage between them. Annette had adopted the respectable title of "the Widow Williams," and although pleased to show Wordsworth their child, she realised, as well as he, that they had now nothing in common save their hatred of Napoleon. For Wordsworth, France had become a country of enemies, and looking back from Calais at the "fair star of evening" stooping over England, he felt more deeply for his country than ever before. But if the visit to France was devoid of warm human relationships it was nevertheless significant as a milestone in his creative development, for it evoked some of the magnificent "*Sonnets Dedicated to Liberty*" which began the greatest period in his poetry.

In the sonnet Wordsworth found his supreme form of expression. The restrictions it imposed

saved him from his faults of prolixity and tediousness, and to their austerity and their splendid
economy of phrase his sonnets largely owe their
pre-eminence. Wordsworth was nearest perfection
when of necessity he dispensed with ornament, and
whereas in a lesser poet this bareness might discover
real barrenness, with Wordsworth it revealed the
chaste beauty of perfect architecture. Now, too,
came the poems which show him striving to learn
bravery from the simple endurance of rustic figures
—*Michael*, *Resolution and Independence*, *The Brothers*.
With his marriage came a further growth in understanding of human experience, although he felt
that he was losing that vision and power which had
previously come to him from nature alone. *To The
Cuckoo*, the opening stanzas of the *Immortality Ode*
and *My Heart Leaps Up* composed within three days
early in 1802, marked the beginning of his sense of
loss. This fading of "the glory and the dream,"
which was really the more acute perception that
he was no longer a child, gave a passionate and
noble poignancy to his poetry.

In 1805, John, the lovable and warm-hearted
sailor brother, was drowned in a shipwreck. For
weeks Wordsworth wrote nothing, but gradually
he settled down to work again, and in May com-
pleted the *Prelude*. Following this he composed
Peele Castle and *The Character of the Happy Warrior*,
that composite portrait whose main inspiration
was John. Wordsworth found peace after his

brother's death in surrender to duty, and *Nuns Fret Not* was probably written at this time.

When William and Dorothy began their life at Grasmere, Coleridge settled at Keswick, and for the next three years they visited each other frequently. Already the fatal disintegration, moral and physical, showed itself in their brilliant and erratic friend. His unhappy relations with his wife, and the deterioration which resulted from the increased use of drugs to alleviate his sufferings were sadly obvious. The three friends began a tour of Scotland together, but after a fortnight, Coleridge's condition compelled him to leave them. The Wordsworths continued their tour, and collected a mass of impressions resulting in Wordsworth's various tributes to Burns, *To A Highland Girl*, *The Solitary Reaper*, *Stepping Westward* and *Yarrow Unvisited*.

Coleridge meanwhile decided to go abroad for his health's sake, and after being nursed through a long illness at Grasmere by Dorothy and Mary he at last set off for Malta. As soon as the electrifying and demanding personality had gone, Wordsworth began work on the *Prelude* which he was writing as a gift for Coleridge. It was nearly three years before they saw him again. Holidays were postponed and plans changed, lest he should arrive while they were away. Finally, he came when they were on holiday at Coleorton in 1807. The shock of his altered appearance was dreadful. His former bright radiance was quite gone, and he was rapidly becoming a morbid, self-centred drug-addict. But ill and changed as he was, he listened rapt while Wordsworth read aloud the *Prelude*.

In this poem are to be found, perfectly blended, that sincerity, lucidity and originality, which are the abiding attributes of Wordsworth's great poetry. Providing, as this great work does, a detailed history of the poet's development, we are given an insight into Wordsworth's mind such as we have into that of no other poet. Thus the *Prelude* is unique among English poems, in that it possesses the double value of art and authenticity. But we cannot talk of art for art's sake as applied to this poem, or indeed to any of Wordsworth's poetry. Wordsworth always wished to be considered a teacher or nothing; he was continuously occupied with moral ideas and frequently lapsed into unashamed didacticism. If we are not interested in the matters which so endlessly concern him, then his poetry is not for us.

By 1806 Wordsworth had three children, John born in 1803, the adored Dora born the following year, and Thomas born in 1806. As Dove Cottage became too small for its occupants and constant stream of visitors—De Quincey, the Coleridges and the Hutchinsons, the family moved in 1808 to Allan Bank, a large new house, where in September Catherine was born. Within a month, Coleridge, now the victim of an elaborate persecution mania, joined them. The previous February he had broken down in London, where Wordsworth had hurried to help him, but in vain. Convinced that his friends were false and treacherous Coleridge wrote letter after letter of bitter criticism. Yet still they tried to salvage the friendship, feeling that he might improve vastly if he would only summon up the courage to separate finally from his wife.

Life at Allan Bank was chaotic, for there was no increase of income to meet the expenses of their larger home. *The White Doe of Rylstone* was finished, but in spite of good reasons urged by Dorothy, Wordsworth refused to consider its publication. Instead he worked over his great *Tract on the Convention of Cintra*, which was published in 1811. Throughout his life he was nearly always reluctant to publish his poems, which is perhaps explained by their consistently poor reception, and when they did appear he professed a stoical indifference to criticism which did not entirely conceal his disappointment.

"The Friend," the venture of Coleridge and Wordsworth into journalism, which was intended to redeem their fortunes, appeared in June, 1808, and continued fitfully until the following March. In bursts of spasmodic energy Coleridge dictated almost the whole periodical to Sara Hutchinson, Mary's sister. Coleridge had fallen in love with this pale, unhappy girl several years before, and now, loved and tormented, she toiled over this work until she departed broken in health and spirit.

Soon afterwards he made the breach between himself and the Wordsworths, towards which he had been driving ever since his return from Malta, and although a kind of reconciliation was effected later they never reached the same intimacy again.

In 1812, two years after their third son William was born, little Catherine died, aged four. The following year, after the death of Thomas, the family moved from the unhealthy house to Rydal Mount, where Wordsworth lived until the end of his life. This was made possible by the poet's obtaining the rather inappropriate office of Distributor of Stamps for Westmoreland. During these restless years he continued to write the *Excursion*, that vast work of industry which occupied him spasmodically for eighteen years until it was concluded in 1814. Its publication was greeted with a critical harshness that was not altogether warranted, for despite dreary wastes of mere didactic versifying it does contain some passages of Miltonic grandeur.

1816-20 has been called the "melancholy period" of Wordsworth's life. He was worried because Richard, who died in 1616, left the family affairs in a chaotic muddle, and the negotiations over his French daughter's marriage settlement were difficult and tedious. He became involved in political activity by becoming a Justice of the Peace and too, was disheartened by the reception of the *Excursion*. This period marked the beginning of a decline in his powers, and during it he produced some of his worst verse. The passionate *Composed upon an Evening of Extraordinary Splendour* written in 1818 bears evidence of his own realisation that the best was past; in this poem he bids farewell to the visionary life.

Although his old age was serene, Wordsworth felt acutely that sadness which is inescapable in one of advanced years. All his friends and some of his family were dead, and, worst of all, Dorothy was condemned since her breakdown in 1829 to twenty-five years of death-in-life. As he grew older Wordsworth leaned more and more towards the orthodox Christian beliefs. The *Ecclesiastical Sonnets* were written in 1821-22. Unfortunately for his poetry he turned from the religion of nature to Church dogma, and became too apt in pointing the moral. His poetry now lacked the sincerity of a vigorous belief either in nature or in Christianity, for he had no secure faith in life after death. "The sunless land" is hardly a prospect of hope, and when Dora died three years before his own death the intensity of his grief bewildered his friends.

Fame came late to Wordsworth; when it did come it was almost overwhelming. Excursion trains were run to Windermere and enthusiasts poured all over his garden. In 1843 on Southey's death he was offered the Laureateship, which after much persuasion he accepted, but honours now meant little to him and four years later, with the death of Dora, he felt that his life was over. Three years afterwards he died.

Much of the common misunderstanding of Wordsworth's poetry comes from mistaking simplicity for *simplesse*. The poet has to walk along a perilous path, and the critic is forever vigilantly watching for him to slip, on the one side into a plethora of metaphor and meaningless obscurity, on the other into over-simplification and tediousness. Unhappily for Wordsworth's reputation he was inclined to overbalance to the side of excessive simplicity and prolixity, making him easy game for the critic. The shallowness of empty high-flown metaphor is perhaps harder to discern than the sterility of uninspired verse, and at least Wordsworth's failing had the virtue of sincerity. From the vast Wordsworthian sands of mediocrity we may pick out many homely brown pebbles, some semi-precious stones, genuine but not flawless, and a few shining diamonds for our lasting delight. These may not glitter with many-faceted brilliance, but they are pellucid, beautiful and enduring.

HELEN DAVIES.

CONTENTS

CONTENTS

CONTENTS

CONTENTS

WRITTEN IN MARCH

The cock is crowing,
The stream is flowing,
The small birds twitter,
The lake doth glitter,
The green field sleeps in the sun;
The oldest and youngest
Are at work with the strongest;
The cattle are grazing,
Their heads never raising;
There are forty feeding like one!

Like an army defeated
The snow hath retreated,
And now doth fare ill
On the top of the bare hill;
The plough-boy is whooping—anon—anon:
There's joy in the mountains;
There's life in the fountains;
Small clouds are sailing,
Blue sky prevailing;
The rain is over and gone!

TO SLEEP

A flock of sheep that leisurely pass by,
One after one; the sound of rain, and bees
Murmuring; the fall of rivers, winds and seas,
Smooth fields, white sheets of water, and pure
    sky;
I have thought of all by turns, and yet do lie
Sleepless, and soon the small birds' melodies
Must hear, first uttered from my orchard trees;
And the first cuckoo's melancholy cry.
Even thus last night, and two nights more, I
    lay,
And could not win thee, sleep! by any stealth;
So do not let me wear to-night away:
Without thee what is all the morning's wealth?
Come, blessed barrier between day and day,
Dear mother of fresh thoughts and joyous
    health!

NUTTING

It seems a day
(I speak of one from many singled out)
One of those heavenly days that cannot die;
When, in the eagerness of boyish hope,
I left our cottage-threshold, sallying forth
With a huge wallet o'er my shoulders slung,
A nutting crook in hand, and turned my steps
Tow'rd some far-distant wood, a figure quaint,
Tricked out in proud disguise of cast-off weeds
Which for that service had been husbanded,
By exhortation of my frugal dame.
Motley accoutrement, of power to smile
At thorns, and brakes, and brambles,—and in truth,
More ragged than need was! O'er pathless rocks,
Through beds of matted fern, and tangled thickets,
Forcing my way, I came to one dear nook
Unvisited, where not a broken bough
Drooped with its withered leaves, ungracious sign
Of devastation, but the hazels rose
Tall and erect, with tempting clusters hung,
A virgin scene!—A little while I stood,
Breathing with such suppression of the heart

As joy delights in; and with wise restraint
Voluptuous, fearless of a rival, eyed
The banquet,—or beneath the trees I sate
Among the flowers, and with the flowers
    played;
A temper known to those, who, after long
And weary expectation, have been blest
With sudden happiness beyond all hope.—
Perhaps it was a bower beneath whose leaves
the violets of five seasons reappear
And fade, unseen by any human eye;
Where faery water-breaks do murmur on
For ever,—and I saw the sparkling foam,
And with my cheek on one of those green stones
That, fleeced with moss, under the shady trees,
Lay round me, scattered like a flock of sheep,
I heard the murmur and the murmuring sound,
In that sweet mood when pleasure loves to pay
Tribute to ease; and, of its joy secure,
The heart luxuriates with indifferent things,
Wasting its kindliness on stocks and stones,
And on the vacant air. Then up I rose,
And dragged to earth both branch and bough,
    with crash
And merciless ravage; and the shady nook
Of hazels, and the green and mossy bower,
Deformed and sullied, patiently gave up
Their quiet being: and, unless I now
Confound my present feelings with the past,

Ere from the mutilated bower I turned
Exulting, rich beyond the wealth of kings,
I felt a sense of pain when I beheld
The silent trees and saw the intruding sky.—
Then, dearest maiden! move along these shades
In gentleness of heart; with gentle hand
Touch—for there is a spirit in the woods.

LONDON, 1802

Milton! thou shouldst be living at this hour:
England hath need of thee; she is a fen
Of stagnant waters; altar, sword and pen,
Fireside, the heroic wealth of hall and bower
Have forfeited their ancient English dower
Of inward happiness. We are selfish men;
Oh! raise us up, return to us again;
And give us manners virtue, freedom, power.
Thou hadst a voice whose sound was like the
    sea;
Pure as the naked heavens, majestic, free,
So didst thou travel on life's common way,
In cheerful godliness; and yet thy heart
The lowliest duties on herself did lay.

THE SOLITARY REAPER

Behold her, single in the field,
Yon solitary Highland lass!
Reaping and singing by herself;
Stop here, or gently pass!
Alone she cuts, and binds the grain,
And sings a melancholy strain;
Oh, listen! for the vale profound
Is overflowing with the sound.

No nightingale did ever chant
More welcome notes to weary bands
Of travellers in some shady haunt,
　Among Arabian sands:
A voice so thrilling ne'er was heard
In spring-time from the cuckoo-bird
Breaking the silence of the seas
Among the farthest Hebrides.

Will no one tell me what she sings?
Perhaps the plaintive numbers flow
For old, unhappy, far-off things,
And battles long ago:
Or is it some more humble lay,
Familiar matter of to-day?
Some natural sorrow, loss, or pain,
That has been, and may be again!

Whate'er the theme, the maiden sang
As if her song could have no ending;
I saw her singing at her work,
And o'er the sickle bending;—
I listened—motionless and still;
And as I mounted up the hill,
The music in my heart I bore,
Long after it was heard no more.

MY HEART LEAPS UP

My heart leaps up when I behold
  A rainbow in the sky:
So was it when my life began;
So is it now I am a man:
So be it when I shall grow old,
  Or let me die!
The child is father of the man;
And I could wish my days to be
Bound each to each by natural piety.

COMPOSED UPON WESTMINSTER BRIDGE
SEPTEMBER 3rd, 1802

Earth has not anything to show more fair:
Dull would he be of soul who could pass by
A sight so touching in its majesty:
This city now doth like a garment wear
The beauty of the morning; silent, bare,
Ships, towers, domes, theatres, and temples lie
Open unto the fields, and to the sky;
All bright and glittering in the smokeless air.
Never did sun more beautifully steep
In his first splendour valley, rock, or hill;
Ne'er saw I, never felt, a calm so deep!
The river glideth at his own sweet will:
Dear God! the very houses seem asleep;
And all that mighty heart is lying still!

A FAREWELL

Farewell, thou little nook of mountain ground,
Thou rocky corner in the lowest stair
Of that magnificent temple which doth bound
One side of our whole vale with grandeur rare;
Sweet garden-orchard, eminently fair,
The loveliest spot that man hath ever found,
Farewell!—we leave thee to heaven's peaceful
 care,
Thee, and the cottage which thou dost sur-
 round.

Our boat is safely anchored by the shore,
And there will safely ride when we are gone;
The flowering shrubs that deck our humble door
Will prosper, though untended and alone.
Fields, goods, and far-off chattels we have none:
These narrow bounds contain our private store
Of things earth makes and sun doth shine upon;
Here are they in our sight—we have no more.

Sunshine and shower be with you, bud and
 bell!
For two months now in vain we shall be sought;
We leave you here in solitude to dwell
With these our latest gifts of tender thought;

Thou, like the morning, in thy saffron coat,
Bright gowan, and marsh-marigold, farewell!
Whom from the borders of the lake we brought,
And placed together near our rocky well.

Dear spot; which we have watched with
      tender heed,
Bringing thee chosen plants and blossoms
      blown
Among the distant mountains, flower and weed,
Which thou hast taken to thee as thy own,
Making all kindness registered and known;

And to soft slumbers, that did gently steep
Our spirits, carrying with them dreams of
      flowers,
And wild notes warbled among leafy bowers;
Two burning months let summer overleap,
And, coming back with her who will be ours,
Into thy bosom we again shall creep.

34

SONNET

The world is too much with us: late and soon,
Getting and spending, we lay waste our powers:
Little we see in nature that is ours;
We have given our hearts away, a sordid boon!
This sea that bares her bosom to the moon:
The winds that will be howling at all hours,
And are up-gathered now like sleeping flowers;
For this, for every thing, we are out of tune;
It moves us not.—Great God! I'd rather be
A pagan suckled in a creed outworn;
So might I, standing on this pleasant lea,
Have glimpses that would make me less for-
    lorn;
Have sight of Proteus rising from the sea;
Or heard old Triton blow his wreathèd horn.

MOUNTAIN ECHOES

'Twas that delightful season when the broom,
Full-flowered, and visible on every steep,
Along the copses runs in veins of gold.
Our pathway led us on to Rotha's banks;
And when we came in front of that tall rock
That eastwards looks, I there stopped short—
   and stood
Tracing the lofty barrier with my eye
From base to summit; such delight I found
To note in shrub and tree, in stone and flower
That intermixture of delicious hues,
Along so vast a surface, all at once,
In one impression, by connecting force
Or their own beauty, imaged in the heart.
When I had gazed perhaps two minutes' space,
Joanna, looking in my eyes, beheld
That ravishment of mine, and laughed aloud.
The rock, like something starting from a sleep,
Took up the lady's voice, and laughed again:
That ancient woman seated on Helm-Crag
Was ready with her cavern: Hammer-Scar,
And the tall steep of Silver-how, sent forth
A noise of laughter; southern Loughrigg heard,
And Fairfield answered with a mountain tone:
Helvellyn far into the clear blue sky

Carried the lady's voice,—old Skiddaw blew
His speaking trumpet;—back out of the clouds
Of Glaramara southward came the voice:
And Kirkstone tossed it from his misty head.

from To Joanna

SONNET

Most sweet it is with unuplifted eyes
To pace the ground if path be there or none,
While a fair region round the traveller lies,
Which he forbears again to look upon;
Pleased rather with some soft ideal scene,
The work of Fancy or some happy tone
Of meditation, slipping in between
The beauty coming and the beauty gone.
If Thought and Love desert us, from that day
Let us break off all commerce with the Muse;
With Thought and Love companions of our
    way,
Whate'er the senses take or may refuse,
The Mind's internal heaven shall shed her dews
Of inspiration on the humblest lay.

THE RAVEN'S NEST

                    Oh! when I have hung
Above the raven's nest, by knots of grass
And half-inch fissures in the slippery rock
But ill sustained, and almost (so it seemed)
Suspended by the blast that blew amain,
Shouldering the naked crag, oh, at that time
While on the perilous ridge I hung alone,
With what strange utterance did the loud dry
    wind
Blow through my ear! the sky seemed not a
    sky
Of earth—and with what motion moved the
    clouds!

from The Prelude, *Book* I

NOVEMBER I

How clear, how keen, how marvellously bright
The effluence from yon distant mountain's
    head,
Which, strewn with snow smooth as the sky
    can shed,
Shines like another sun—on mortal sight
Uprisen, as if to check approaching night,
And all her twinkling stars. Who now would
    tread,
If so he might, yon mountain's glittering
    head—
Terrestrial—but a surface, by the flight
Of sad mortality's earth-sullying wing,
Unswept, unstained! Nor shall the aërial
    powers
Dissolve that beauty—destined to endure,
White, radiant, spotless, exquisitely pure,
Through all vicissitudes—till genial spring
Has filled the laughing vales with welcome
    flowers.

39

FROM JOY TO SORROW

There was a roaring in the wind all night;
The rain came heavily, and fell in floods;
But now the sun is rising calm and bright;
The birds are singing in the distant woods;
Over his own sweet voice the stockdove broods;
The jay makes answer as the magpie chatters;
And all the air is filled with pleasant noise of
 waters.

All things that love the sun are out of doors:
The sky rejoices in the morning's birth;
The grass is bright with rain-drops;—on the
 moors
The hare is running races in her mirth;
And with her feet she from the plashy earth
Raises a mist; that, glittering in the sun,
Runs with her all the way, wherever she doth run.

I was a traveller then upon the moor;
I saw the hare that raced about with joy;
I heard the woods and distant waters roar,
Or heard them not as happy as a boy:
The pleasant season, did my heart employ:
My old remembrances went from me wholly;
And all the ways of men so vain and melan-
 choly!

But, as it sometimes chanceth, from the
    might
Of joy in minds that can no further go,
As high as we have mounted in delight
In our dejection do we sink as low,
To me that morning did it happen so;
And fears, and fancies, thick upon me
    came;
Dim sadness—and blind thoughts, I knew not,
    nor could name.

I heard the sky-lark warbling in the sky;
And I bethought me of the playful hare:
Even such a happy child of earth am I;
Even as these blissful creatures do I fare;
Far from the world I walk, and from all
    care;
But there may come another day to me—
Solitude, pain of heart, distress, and poverty.

My whole life I have lived in pleasant thought,
As if life's business were a summer mood;
As if all needful things would come unsought
To genial faith, still rich in genial good;
But how can he expect that others should
Build for him, sow for him, and at his
    call
Love him, who for himself will take no heed
    at all?

I thought of Chatterton, the marvellous boy,
The sleepless soul that perished in his pride;
Of him who walked in glory and in joy
Following his plough, along the mountain-
    side:
By our own spirits are we deified
We poets in our youth begin in gladness;
But thereof come in the end despondency and
    madness.

from Resolution and Independence

ON THE BANKS OF A ROCKY STREAM

Behold an emblem of our human mind
Crowded with thoughts that need a settled
    home,
Yet, like to eddying balls of foam
Within this whirlpool, they each other chase
Round and round, and neither find
An outlet nor a resting place!
Stranger, if such disquietude be thine.
Fall on thy knees and sue for help divine.

SONNET

Surprised by joy—impatient as the wind
I turned to share the transport—Oh! with
whom
But thee deep buried in the silent tomb,
That spot which no vicissitude can find,
Love, faithful love, recalled thee to my mind—
But how could I forget?—Through what
power,
Even for the least division of an hour,
Have I been so beguiled as to be blind
To my most grievous loss?—That thought's
return
Was the worst pang that sorrow ever bore,
Save one, one only, when I stood forlorn,
Knowing my heart's best treasure was no more;
That neither present time, nor years unborn
Could to my sight that heavenly face restore.

CHARACTER OF THE HAPPY WARRIOR

Who is the happy warrior? Who is he
That every man in arms should wish to be?
It is the generous spirit, who, when brought
Among the tasks of real life, hath wrought
Upon the plan that pleased his boyish
    thought:
Whose high endeavours are an inward light
That makes the path before him always bright:
Who, with a natural instinct to discern
What knowledge can perform, is diligent to
    learn;
Abides by this resolve, and stops not there,
But makes his moral being his prime care;
Who, doomed to go in company with pain,
And fear, and bloodshed, miserable train!
Turns his necessity to glorious gain;
In face of these doth exercise a power
Which is our human nature's highest dower;
Controls them and subdues, transmutes,
    bereaves,
Of their bad influence, and their good receives;
By objects, which might force the soul to abate
Her feeling, rendered more compassionate;
Is placable—because occasions rise
So often that demand such sacrifice;

More skilful in self-knowledge, even more
    pure,
As tempted more; more able to endure,
As more exposed to suffering and distress;
Thence, also, more alive to tenderness.
'Tis he whose law is reason; who depends
Upon that law as on the best of friends;
Whence, in a state where men are tempted still
To evil for a guard against worse ill,
And what in quality or act is best
Doth seldom on a right foundation rest,
He labours good on good to fix, and owes
To virtue every triumph that he knows;
Who, if he rise to station of command,
Rises by open means; and there will stand
On honourable terms, or else retire,
And in himself possess his own desire;
Who comprehends his trust, and to the same
Keeps faithful with a singleness of aim;
And therefore does not stoop, nor lie in wait
For wealth, or honours, or for worldly state;
Whom they must follow; on whose head must
    fall,
Like showers of manna, if they come at all:
Whose powers shed round him in the common
    strife,
Or mild concerns of ordinary life,
A constant influence, a peculiar grace;
But who, if he be called upon to face

Some awful moment to which Heaven has
    joined
Great issues, good or bad for human kind,
Is happy as a lover; and attired
With sudden brightness, like a man inspired;
And, through the heat of conflict, keeps the law
In calmness made, and sees what he foresaw;
Or if an unexpected call succeed,
Come when it will, is equal to the need:
He who though thus endued as with a sense
And faculty for storm and turbulence,
Is yet a soul whose master-bias leans
To homefelt pleasures and to gentle scenes;
Sweet images! which, whereso 'er he be,
Are at his heart; and such fidelity
It is his darling passion to approve;
More brave for this, that he hath much to
    love:—
'Tis, finally, the man, who, lifted high,
Conspicuous object in a nation's eye,
Or left unthought-of in obscurity,—
Who, with a toward or untoward lot,
Prosperous or adverse, to his wish or not,
Plays, in the many games of life, that one
Where what he most doth value must be won:
Whom neither shape of danger can dismay,
Nor thought of tender happiness betray;
Who, not content that former worth stand fast,
Looks forward, persevering to the last,

46

From well to better, daily self-surpast:
Who, whether praise of him must walk the earth
For ever, and to noble deeds give birth,
Or he must fall, to sleep without his fame,
And leave a dead unprofitable name,
Finds comfort in himself and in his cause;
And, while the mortal mist is gathering, draws
His breath in confidence of Heaven's applause:
This is the happy warrior; this is he
That every man in arms should wish to be.

SONNET

It is a beauteous evening, calm and free;
The holy time is quiet as a nun
Breathless with adoration; the broad sun
Is sinking down in its tranquillity;
The gentleness of heaven broods o'er the sea:
Listen! the mighty Being is awake,
And doth with His eternal motion make
A sound like thunder—everlastingly.
Dear child! dear girl! that walkest with me
        here,
If thou appear untouched by solemn thought,
Thy nature is not therefore less divine:
Thou liest in Abraham's bosom all the year;
And worship'st at the temple's inner shrine,
God being with thee when we know it not.

47

DAFFODILS

I wandered lonely as a cloud
That floats on high o'er vales and hills,
When all at once I saw a crowd,
A host of golden daffodils;
Beside the lake, beneath the trees,
Fluttering and dancing in the breeze.

Continuous as the stars that shine
And twinkle on the milky way,
They stretched in never-ending line
Along the margin of a bay:
Ten thousand saw I at a glance,
Tossing their heads in sprightly dance.

The waves beside them danced, but they
Outdid the sparkling waves in glee:—
A poet could not but be gay,
In such a jocund company:
I gazed—and gazed—but little thought
What wealth the show to me had brought:

For oft when on my couch I lie
In vacant or in pensive mood,
They flash upon that inward eye
Which is the bliss of solitude,
And then my heart with pleasure fills,
And dances with the daffodils.

COMPOSED BY THE SEA-SIDE, NEAR CALAIS,
AUGUST, 1802

Fair star of evening, splendour of the west,
Star of my country!—on the horizon's brink
Thou hangest, stooping, as might seem, to sink
On England's bosom: yet well pleased to rest,
Meanwhile, and be to her a glorious crest
Conspicuous to the nations. Thou, I think,
Shouldst be my country's emblem; and
    shouldst wink,
Bright star! with laughter on her banners,
    drest
In thy fresh beauty. There! that dusky spot
Beneath thee, that is England; there she lies.
Blessings be on you both! one hope, one lot,
One life, one glory! I with many a fear
For my dear country, many heartfelt sighs,
Among men who do not love her, linger here.

LINES

*Composed a few miles above Tintern Abbey, on
revisiting the banks of the Wye during a tour,
July 13, 1798.*

Five years have past; five summers, with the
    length
Of five long winters! and again I hear
These waters, rolling from their mountain
    springs
With a sweet inland murmur.[1]—Once again
Do I behold these steep and lofty cliffs,
That on a wild secluded scene impress
Thoughts of more deep seclusion; and connect
The landscape with the quiet of the sky.
The day is come when I again repose
Here, under this dark sycamore, and view
These plots of cottage-ground, these orchard-
    tufts,
Which at this season, with their unripe fruits,
Are clad in one green hue, and lose themselves
'Mid groves and copses. Once again I see
These hedgerows, hardly hedgerows, little lines
Of sportive wood run wild; these pastoral
    farms,
Green to the very door; and wreaths of smoke
Sent up in silence, from among the trees!

[1] The river is not affected by the tides a few miles above Tintern.

With some uncertain notice, as might seem,
Of vagrant dwellers in the houseless woods,
Or of some hermit's cave, where by his fire
The hermit sits alone.
                    These beauteous forms,
Through a long absence, have not been to me
As is a landscape to a blind man's eye:
But oft, in lonely rooms, and 'mid the din
Of towns and cities, I have owed to them,
In hours of weariness, sensations sweet,
Felt in the blood, and felt along the heart;
And passing even into my purer mind,
With tranquil restoration:—feelings, too,
Of unremembered pleasure: such, perhaps,
As have no slight or trivial influence
On that best portion of a good man's life,
His little, nameless, unremembered acts
Of kindness and of love. Nor less, I trust,
To them I may have owed another gift,
Of aspect more sublime; that blessed mood,
In which the burthen of the mystery,
In which the heavy and the weary weight
Of all this unintelligible world,
Is lightened:—that serene and blessed mood,
In which the affections gently lead us on,—
Until, the breath of this corporeal frame,
And even the motion of our human blood
Almost suspended, we are laid asleep
In body, and become a living soul:

While with an eye made quiet by the power
Of harmony, and the deep power of joy,
We see into the life of things.

                              If this
Be but a vain belief, yet, oh! how oft—
In darkness, and amid the many shapes
Of joyless daylight; when the fretful stir
Unprofitable, and the fever of the world,
Have hung upon the beatings of my heart,
How oft, in spirit, have I turned to thee,
O sylvan Wye! Thou wanderer through the
     woods,
How often has my spirit turned to thee!
And now, with gleams of half-extinguished
     thought,
With many recognitions dim and faint,
And somewhat of a sad perplexity,
The picture of the mind revives again:
While here I stand, not only with the sense
Of present pleasure, but with pleasing thoughts
That in this moment there is life and food
For future years. And so I dare to hope,
Though changed, no doubt, from what I was
     when first
I came among these hills; when like a roe
I bounded o'er the mountains, by the sides
Of the deep rivers, and the lonely streams,
Wherever nature led: more like a man
Flying from something that he dreads, than one

Who sought the thing he loved. For nature
then
(The coarser pleasures of my boyish days
And their glad animal movements all gone by)
To me was all in all.—I cannot paint
What then I was. The sounding cataract
Haunted me like a passion: the tall rock
The mountain, and the deep and gloomy wood,
Their colours and their forms, were then to me
An appetite: a feeling and a love,
That had no need of a remoter charm,
By thought supplied, or any interest
Unborrowed from the eye.—That time is past,
And all its aching joys are now no more
And all its dizzy raptures. Not for this
Faint I, nor mourn nor murmur; other gifts
Have followed, for such loss, I would believe,
Abundant recompense. For I have learned
To look on nature, not as in the hour
Of thoughtless youth; but hearing oftentimes
The still, sad music of humanity,
Nor harsh nor grating, though of ample power
To chasten and subdue. And I have felt
A presence that disturbs me with the joy
Of elevated thoughts; a sense sublime
Of something far more deeply interfused,
Whose dwelling is the light of setting suns,
And the round ocean, and the living air,
And the blue sky, and in the mind of man:

A motion and a spirit, that impels
All thinking things, all objects of all thought,
And rolls through all things. Therefore am I
    still
A lover of the meadows and the woods,
And mountains; and of all that we behold
From this green earth; of all the mighty world
Of eye and ear, both what they half create,
And what perceive; well pleased to recognise
In nature and the language of the sense,
The anchor of my purest thoughts, the nurse,
The guide, the guardian of my heart, and soul
Of all my moral being.
               Nor perchance,
If I were not thus taught, should I the more
Suffer my genial spirits to decay:
For thou art with me, here upon the banks
Of this fair river; thou, my dearest friend,
My dear, dear friend, and in thy voice I catch
The language of my former heart, and read
My former pleasures in the shooting lights
Of thy wild eyes. Oh! yet a little while
May I behold in thee what I was once,
My dear, dear sister! and this prayer I make,
Knowing that nature never did betray
The heart that loved her; 'tis her privilege,
Through all the years of this our life, to lead
From joy to joy: for she can so inform
The mind that is within us, so impress

With quietness and beauty, and so feed
With lofty thoughts, that neither evil tongues
Rash judgments, nor the sneers of selfish men,
Nor greetings where no kindness is, nor all
The dreary intercourse of daily life,
Shall e'er prevail against us, or disturb
Our cheerful faith, that all which we behold
Is full of blessings. Therefore let the moon
Shine on thee in thy solitary walk;
And let the misty mountain winds be free
To blow against thee: and, in after years,
When these wild ecstasies shall be matured
Into a sober pleasure, when thy mind
Shall be a mansion for all lovely forms,
Thy memory be as a dwelling-place
For all sweet sounds and harmonies; oh! then,
If solitude, or fear, or pain, or grief,
Should be thy portion, with what healing
        thoughts
Of tender joy wilt thou remember me,
And these my exhortations! Nor, perchance—
If I should be where I no more can hear
Thy voice, nor catch from thy wild eyes these
        gleams
Of past existence—wilt thou then forget
That on the banks of this delightful stream
We stood together; and that I, so long
A worshipper of nature, hither came,
Unwearied in that service: rather say

With warmer love—oh! with far deeper zeal
Of holier love. Nor wilt thou then forget,
That after many wanderings, many years
Of absence, these steep woods and lofty cliffs,
And this green pastoral landscape, were to me
More dear, both for themselves and for thy
    sake!

SONNET

With how sad steps, O moon, thou climb'st the
    sky,
"How silently, and with how wan a face!"
Where art thou? Thou so often seen on high
Running among the clouds a wood-nymph's
    race!
Unhappy nuns, whose common breath's a sigh
Which they would stifle, move at such a pace!
The northern wind, to call thee to the chase,
Must blow to-night his bugle horn. Had I
The power of Merlin, goddess! this should be;
And all the stars, fast as the clouds were riven,
Should sally forth, to keep thee company,
Hurrying and sparkling through the clear blue
    heaven;
But Cynthia! should to thee the palm be given,
Queen both for beauty and for majesty.

THE GREEN LINNET

Beneath these fruit-tree boughs that shed
Their snow-white blossoms on my head,
With brightest sunshine round me spread
  Of spring's unclouded weather,
In this sequestered nook how sweet
To sit upon my orchard-seat!
And birds and flowers once more to greet,
  My last year's friends together.

One have I marked, the happiest guest
In all this covert of the blest;
Hail to thee, far above the rest
  In joy of voice and pinion,
Thou, linnet! in thy green array,
Presiding spirit here to-day,
Dost lead the revels of the May,
  And this is thy dominion.

While birds and butterflies, and flowers
Make all one band of paramours,
Thou, ranging up and down the bowers,
  Art sole in thy employment;
A life, a presence like the air,
Scattering thy gladness without care,
Too blest with any one to pair,
  Thyself thy own enjoyment.

Amid yon tuft of hazel trees,
That twinkle to the gusty breeze,
Behold him perched in ecstasies,
   Yet seeming still to hover;
There! where the flutter of his wings
Upon his back and body flings
Shadows and sunny glimmerings,
   That cover him all over.

My dazzled sight he oft deceives,
A brother of the dancing leaves;
Then flits, and from the cottage eaves
   Pours forth his song in gushes;
As if by that exulting strain
He mocked and treated with disdain
The voiceless form he chose to feign,
   While fluttering in the bushes.

THE SUBJUGATION OF SWITZERLAND

Two voices are there; one is of the sea,
One of the mountains; each a mighty voice.
In both from age to age thou didst rejoice,
They were thy chosen music, liberty!
There came a tyrant, and with holy glee
Thou fought'st against him; but hast vainly
    striven.
Thou from thy Alpine holds at length art
    driven,
Where not a torrent murmurs heard by thee.
Of one deep bliss thine ear hath been bereft;
Then cleave, oh, cleave to that which still is
    left;
For, high-souled maid, what sorrow would it be
That mountain floods should thunder as before,
And ocean bellow from his rocky shore,
And neither awful voice be heard by thee!

LINES

Composed at Grasmere, during a walk one Evening,
after a stormy day, the Author having just read in a
Newspaper that the dissolution of Mr. Fox was
hourly expected.

Loud is the Vale! the Voice is up
With which she speaks when storms are gone,
A mighty unison of streams!
Of all her Voices, One!

Loud is the Vale;—this inland Depth
In peace is roaring like the Sea;
Yon star upon the mountain-top
Is listening quietly.

Sad was I, even to pain deprest,
Importunate and heavy load!
The Comforter hath found me here
Upon this lonely road;

And many thousands now are sad—
Wait the fulfilment of their fear;
For he must die who is their stay,
Their glory disappear.

A Power is passing from the earth
To breathless Nature's dark abyss;
But when the great and good depart
What is it more than this—

That Man, who is from God sent forth,
Doth yet again to God return?—
Such ebb and flow must ever be,
Then wherefore should we mourn?

SONNET

When I have borne in memory what has tamed
Great nations, how ennobling thoughts depart
When men change swords for ledgers, and desert
The student's bower for gold, some fears un-
        named
I had, my country!—am I to be blamed?
Now, when I think of thee, and what thou art,
Verily, in the bottom of my heart,
Of those unfilial fears I am ashamed.
For dearly must we prize thee; we who find
In thee a bulwark for the cause of men;
And I by my affection was beguiled.
What wonder if a poet now and then,
Among the many movements of his mind,
Felt for thee as a lover or a child?

DANCE OF THE WIND

A whirl-blast from behind the hill
Rushed o'er the wood with startling sound;
Then—all at once the air was still,
And showers of hailstones pattered round.
Where leafless oaks towered high above,
I sat within an undergrove
Of tallest hollies, tall and green;
A fairer bower was never seen.
From year to year the spacious floor
With withered leaves is covered o'er,
And all the year the bower is green.
But see! where'er the hailstones drop,
The withered leaves all skip and hop,
There's not a breeze—no breath of air—
Yet here, and there, and every where
Along the floor, beneath the shade
By those embowering hollies made,
The leaves in myriads jump and spring,
As if with pipes and music rare
Some Robin Good-fellow were there,
And all those leaves, in festive glee,
Were dancing to the minstrelsy.

SONNET

A volant tribe of bards on earth are found,
Who, while the flattering zephyrs round them
    play,
On "coignes of vantage" hang their nests of
    clay;
How quickly from that aery hold unbound,
Dust for oblivion! To the solid ground
Of nature trusts the mind that builds for aye;
Convinced that there, there only, she can lay
Secure foundations. As the year runs round,
Apart she toils within the chosen ring;
While the stars shine, or while day's purple eye
Is gently closing with the flowers of spring;
Where even the motion of an angel's wing
Would interrupt the intense tranquillity
Of silent hills, and more than silent sky.

THE WHITE DOE

A moment ends the fervent din,
And all is hushed, without and within;
For though the priest, more tranquilly,
Recites the holy liturgy,
The only voice which you can hear
Is the river murmuring near.
When soft!—the dusky trees between,
And down the path through the open green,
Where is no living thing to be seen;
And through yon gateway, where is found,
Beneath the arch with ivy bound,
Free entrance to the church-yard ground;
Comes gliding in with lovely gleam,
Comes gliding in serene and slow,
Soft and silent as a dream,
A solitary doe!
White she is as lily of June,
And beauteous as the silver moon
When out of sight the clouds are driven,
And she is left alone in heaven;
Or like a ship some gentle day
In sunshine sailing far away,
A glittering ship, that hath the plain
Of ocean for her own domain.

  ·   ·   ·   ·   ·   ·

But hers are eyes serenely bright,
And on she moves—with pace how light?
Nor spares to stoop her head, and taste
The dewy turf with flowers bestrown;
And thus she fares, until at last
Beside the ridge of a grassy grave
In quietness she lays her down;
Gently as a weary wave
Sinks, when the summer breeze hath died,
Against an anchored vessel's side;
Even so, without distress, doth she
Lie down in peace, and lovingly.

from The White Doe of Rylstone

MEMORY

And when the stream
Which overflowed the soul was passed away,
A consciousness remained that it had left,
Deposited upon the silent shore
Of memory, images and precious thoughts
That shall not die, and cannot be destroyed.

from The Excursion

ON THE EXTINCTION OF THE VENETIAN REPUBLIC

Once did she hold the gorgeous East in fee;
And was the safeguard of the west: the worth
Of Venice did not fall below her birth,
Venice, the eldest child of liberty.
She was a maiden city, bright and free;
No guile seduced, no force could violate;
And when she took unto herself a mate,
She must espouse the everlasting sea!
And what if she had seen those glories fade,
Those titles vanish, and that strength decay;
Yet shall some tribute of regret be paid
When her long life hath reached its final day:
Men are we, and must grieve when even the
    shade
Of that which once was great, is passed away.

ANIMAL TRANQUILLITY AND DECAY

The little hedgerow birds,
That peck along the road, regard him not,
He travels on, and in his face, his step,
His gait, is one expression: every limb,
His look and bending figure, all bespeak
A man who does not move with pain, but moves
With thought.—He is insensibly subdued
To settled quiet: he is one by whom
All effort seems forgotten; one to whom
Long patience hath such mild composure given,
That patience now doth seem a thing of which
He hath no need. He is by nature led
To peace so perfect that the young behold
With envy, what the Old Man hardly feels.

SONNET

I watch, and long have watched, with calm
    regret
Yon slowly-sinking star—immortal Sire
(So might he seem) of all the glittering quire!
Blue ether still surrounds him—yet—and yet;
But now the horizon's rocky parapet
Is reached, where, forfeiting his bright attire,
He burns—transmuted to a dusky fire—
Then pays submissively the appointed debt
To the flying moments, and is seen no more.
Angels and gods! We struggle with out fate,
While health, power, glory, from their height
    decline,
Depressed; and then extinguished: and our
    state,
In this, how different, lost Star, from thine,
That no to-morrow shall our beams restore!

YES, THOU ART FAIR

Yes! thou art fair, yet be not moved
  To scorn the declaration,
That sometimes I in thee have loved
  My fancy's own creation.

Imagination needs must stir;
  Dear Maid, this truth believe,
Minds that have nothing to confer
  Find little to perceive.

Be pleased that nature made thee fit
  To feed my heart's devotion,
By laws to which all Forms submit
  In sky, air, earth, and ocean.

SONNET

Who swerves from innocence, who makes
    divorce
Of that serene companion—a good name,
Recovers not his loss; but walks with shame,
With doubt, with fear, and haply with remorse.
And oft-times he, who, yielding to the force
Of chance temptation, ere his journey end,
From chosen comrade turns, or faithful friend,
In vain shall rue the broken intercourse.
Not so with such as loosely wear the chain
That binds them, pleasant river! to thy side:—
Through the rough copse wheel thou with
    hasty stride,
I choose to saunter o'er the grassy plain,
Sure, when the separation has been tried,
That we, who part in love, shall meet again.

FIVE POEMS RELATING TO LUCY

I

I travelled among unknown men,
  In lands beyond the sea;
Nor, England! did I know till then
  What love I bore to thee.

'Tis past, that melancholy dream!
  Nor will I quit thy shore
A second time; for still I seem
  To love thee more and more.

Among thy mountains did I feel
  The joy of my desire;
And she I cherished turned her wheel
  Beside an English fire.

Thy mornings showed, thy nights concealed
  The bowers where Lucy played;
And thine too is the last green field
  That Lucy's eyes surveyed.

71

2

Three years she grew in sun and shower
Then nature said, "A lovelier flower
On earth was never sown;
This child I to myself will take;
She shall be mine, and I will make
A lady of my own.

"Myself will to my darling be
Both law and impulse: and with me
The girl, in rock and plain,
In earth and heaven, in glade and bower,
Shall feel an overseeing power
To kindle or restrain.

"She shall be sportive as the fawn
That wild with glee across the lawn
Or up the mountain springs;
And hers shall be the breathing balm,
And hers the silence and the calm
Of mute insensate things.

"The floating clouds their state shall lend
To her; for her the willow bend:
Nor shall she fail to see
Even in the motions of the storm
Grace that shall mould the maiden's form
By silent sympathy.

"The stars of midnight shall be dear
To her; and she shall lean her ear
In many a secret place
Where rivulets dance their wayward round,
And beauty born of murmuring sound
Shall pass into her face.

"And vital feelings of delight
Shall rear her form to stately height,
Her virgin bosom swell;
Such thoughts to Lucy I will give
While she and I together live
Here in this happy dell."

Thus nature spake—the work was done—
How soon my Lucy's race was run!
She died, and left to me
This heath, this calm and quiet scene;
The memory of what has been,
And never more will be.

3

A slumber did my spirit seal;
   I had no human fears:
She seemed a thing that could not feel
   The touch of earthly years.

No motion has she now, no force;
   She neither hears nor sees,
Rolled round in earth's diurnal course,
   With rocks and stones and trees!

4

She dwelt among the untrodden ways
   Beside the springs of Dove,
A maid whom there were none to praise,
   And very few to love.

A violet by a mossy stone
   Half-hidden from the eye!
Fair as a star, when only one
   Is shining in the sky.

She lived unknown, and few could know
   When Lucy ceased to be;
But she is in her grave, and, oh,
   The difference to me!

5

She was a phantom of delight
When first she gleamed upon my sight
A lovely apparition, sent
To be a moment's ornament;
Her eyes as stars of twilight fair;
Like twilight's too, her dusky hair;
But all things else about her drawn
From May-time and the cheerful dawn;
A dancing shape, an image gay,
To haunt, to startle, and waylay.

I saw her upon nearer view,
A spirit, yet a woman too!
Her household motions light and free,
And steps of virgin liberty;
A countenance in which did meet
Sweet records, promises as sweet;
A creature not too bright or good
For human nature's daily food;
For transient sorrows, simple wiles,
Praise, blame, love, kisses, tears, and smiles.

And now I see with eye serene
The very pulse of the machine;
A being breathing thoughtful breath,
A traveller between life and death;
The reason firm, the temperate will,

75

Endurance, foresight, strength, and skill,
A perfect woman, nobly planned,
To warn, to comfort, and command;
And yet a spirit still, and bright
With something of angelic light.

AMONG ALL LOVELY THINGS

Among all lovely things my Love had been;
Had noted well the stars, all flowers that grew
About her home; but she had never seen
A Glow-worm, never one, and this I knew.

While riding near her home one stormy night
A single Glow-worm did I chance to espy;
I gave a fervent welcome to the sight,
And from my Horse I leapt; great joy had I.

Upon a leaf the Glow-worm did I lay,
To bear it with me through the stormy night:
And, as before, it shone without dismay;
Albeit putting forth a fainter light.

When to the Dwelling of my Love I came,
I went into the Orchard quietly;
And left the Glow-worm, blessing it by name,
Laid safely by itself, beneath a Tree.

The whole next day, I hoped, and hoped with
    fear;
At night the Glow-worm shone beneath the
    Tree:
I led my Lucy to the spot, "Look here!"
Oh! joy it was for her, and joy for me!

IF THIS GREAT WORLD

If this great world of joy and pain
    Revolve in one sure track;
If Freedom, set, will rise again,
    And Virtue, flown, come back;
Woe to the purblind crew who fill
    The heart with each day's care;
Nor gain, from past or future, skill
    To bear, and to forbear!

SONNET

Why art thou silent! Is thy love a plant
Of such weak fibre that the treacherous air
Of absence withers what was once so fair?
Is there no debt to pay, no boon to grant?
Yet have my thoughts for thee been vigilant
Bound to thy service with unceasing care,
The mind's least generous wish a mendicant.
For naught but what thy happiness could spare.
Speak, though this soft warm heart, once free
    to hold
A thousand tender pleasures, thine and mine,
Be left more desolate, more dreary cold
Than a forsaken bird's-nest filled with snow
'Mid its own bush of leafless eglantine;
Speak, that my torturing doubts their end may
    know!

ODE

INTIMATIONS OF IMMORTALITY FROM
RECOLLECTIONS OF EARLY CHILDHOOD

The Child is father of the Man:
And I could wish my days to be
Bound each to each by natural piety.

I

There was a time when meadow, grove, and
    stream,
The earth, and every common sight,
    To me did seem
    Apparelled in celestial light,
The glory and the freshness of a dream.
It is not now as it hath been of yore;—
    Turn wheresoe'er I may,
      By night or day,
The things which I have seen I now can see no
    more.

2

    The Rainbow comes and goes,
    And lovely is the Rose;
    The Moon doth with delight
Look round her when the heavens are bare;
    Waters on a starry night
    Are beautiful and fair;

The sunshine is a glorious birth;
But yet I know, where'er I go,
That there hath past away a glory from the
earth.

3

Now, while the birds thus sing a joyous song,
And while the young lambs bound
As to the tabor's sound,
To me alone there came a thought of grief:
A timely utterance gave that thought relief,
And I again am strong:
The cataracts blow their trumpets from the
steep;
No more shall grief of mine the season wrong;
I hear the Echoes through the mountains
throng,
The Winds come to me from the fields of sleep,
And all the earth is gay;
Land and sea
Give themselves up to jollity,
And with the heart of May
Doth every Beast keep holiday;—
Thou Child of Joy,
Shout round me, let me hear thy shouts, thou
happy Shepherd-boy!

4

Ye blessèd Creatures, I have heard the call
   Ye to each other make; I see
The heavens laugh with you in your jubilee;
   My heart is at your festival,
   My head hath its coronal,
The fullness of your bliss, I feel—I feel it all.
      Oh evil day! if I were sullen
      While Earth herself is adorning,
         This sweet May-morning,
      And the Children are culling
         On every side,
      In a thousand valleys far and wide,
      Fresh flowers; while the sun shines warm,
And the Babe leaps up on his Mother's arm:—
      I hear, I hear, with joy I hear!
      —But there's a Tree, of many, one,
A single Field which I have looked upon,
Both of them speak of something that is gone:
         The Pansy at my feet
         Doth the same tale repeat:
Whither is fled the visionary gleam?
Where is it now, the glory and the dream?

5

Our birth is but a sleep and a forgetting:
The Soul that rises with us, our life's Star,
   Hath had elsewhere its setting,
    And cometh from afar:
   Not in entire forgetfulness,
   And not in utter nakedness,
But trailing clouds of glory do we come
   From God, who is our home:
Heaven lies about us in our infancy!
Shades of the prison-house begin to close
   Upon the growing Boy,
But He beholds the light, and whence it flows,
   He sees it in his joy;
The Youth, who daily farther from the east
   Must travel, still is Nature's Priest,
    And by the vision splendid
    Is on his way attended;
At length the Man perceives it die away,
And fade into the light of common day.

6

Earth fills her lap with pleasures of her own;
Yearnings she hath in her own natural kind,
And, even with something of a Mother's mind,

And no unworthy aim,
　The homely Nurse doth all she can
To make her Foster-child, her Inmate Man,
　　Forget the glories he hath known,
And that imperial palace whence he came.

7

Behold the Child among his new-born blisses,
A six years' Darling of a pigmy size!
See, where 'mid work of his own hand he
　　lies,
Fretted by sallies of his mother's kisses,
With light upon him from his father's eyes!
See, at his feet, some little plan or chart,
Some fragment from his dream of human
　　life,
Shaped by himself with newly-learned art;
　　A wedding or a festival,
　　A mourning or a funeral;
　　　And this hath now his heart,
　　And unto this he frames his song:
　　　Then will he fit his tongue
To dialogues of business, love, or strife;
　　But it will not be long
　　Ere this be thrown aside,
　　And with new joy and pride
The little Actor cons another part;

Filling from time to time his "humorous
    stage"
With all the Persons, down to palsied Age,
That Life brings with her in her equipage;
    As if his whole vocation
    Were endless imitation.

8

Thou, whose exterior semblance doth belie
    Thy Soul's immensity;
Thou best Philosopher, who yet dost keep
Thy heritage, thou Eye among the blind,
That, deaf and silent, read'st the eternal deep,
Haunted for ever by the eternal mind,—
    Mighty Prophet! Seer blest!
    On whom those truths do rest,
Which we are toiling all our lives to find,
In darkness lost, the darkness of the grave;
Thou, over whom thy Immortality
Broods like the Day, a Master o'er a Slave,
A Presence which is not to be put by;
    [To whom the grave
Is but a lonely bed without the sense of sight
    Of day or the warm light,
A place of thought where we in waiting lie;]
Thou little Child, yet glorious in the might
Of heaven-born freedom on thy being's height,

Why with such earnest pains dost thou provoke
The years to bring the inevitable yoke,
Thus blindly with thy blessedness at strife?
Full soon thy Soul shall have her earthly
    freight,
And custom lie upon thee with a weight,
Heavy as frost, and deep almost as life!

9

O joy! that in our embers
Is something that doth live,
That nature yet remembers
What was so fugitive!
The thought of our past years in me doth breed
Perpetual benediction: not indeed
For that which is most worthy to be blest;
Delight and liberty, the simple creed
Of Childhood, whether busy or at rest,
With new-fledged hope still fluttering in his
    breast:—
Not for these I raise
The song of thanks and praise;
But for those obstinate questionings
Of sense and outward things,
Fallings from us, banishings;
Blank misgivings of a Creature
Moving about in worlds not realised,

High instincts before which our mortal Nature
Did tremble like a guilty Thing surprised:
    But for those first affections,
    Those shadowy recollections,
        Which, be they what they may,
Are yet the fountain-light of all our day,
Are yet a master-light of all our seeing;
        Uphold us, cherish, and have power to
            make
Our noisy years seem moments in the being
Of the eternal Silence: truths that wake,
        To perish never:
Which neither listlessness, nor mad endeavour,
        Nor Man nor Boy,
Nor all that is at enmity with joy,
Can utterly abolish or destroy!
    Hence in a season of calm weather
        Though inland far we be,
Our Souls have sight of that immortal sea
        Which brought us hither,
    Can in a moment travel thither,
And see the Children sport upon the shore,
And hear the mighty waters rolling evermore.

10

Then sing, ye Birds, sing, sing a joyous song!
    And let the young Lambs bound
    As to the tabor's sound!
We in thought will join your throng,
    Ye that pipe and ye that play,
    Ye that through your hearts to-day
    Feel the gladness of the May!
What though the radiance which was once so
      bright
Be now for ever taken from my sight,
  Though nothing can bring back the hour
Of splendour in the grass, of glory in the
      flower;
    We will grieve not, rather find
    Strength in what remains behind;
    In the primal sympathy
    Which having been must ever be;
    In the soothing thoughts that spring
    Out of human suffering;
    In the faith that looks through death,
In years that bring the philosophic mind.

II

And O, ye Fountains, Meadows, Hills, and
      Groves,
Forebode not any severing of our loves!
Yet in my heart of hearts I feel your might;
I only have relinquished one delight
To live beneath your more habitual sway.
I love the Brooks which down their channels
      fret,
Even more than when I tripped lightly as they;
The innocent brightness of a new-born Day
      Is lovely yet;
The Clouds that gather round the setting sun
Do take a sober colouring from an eye
That hath kept watch o'er man's mortality;
Another race hath been, and other palms are
      won.
Thanks to the human heart by which we live,
Thanks to its tenderness, its joys, and fears,
To me the meanest flower that blows can give
Thoughts that do often lie too deep for tears.

SONNET

It is not to be thought of that the flood
Of British freedom, which, to the open sea
Of the world's praise, from dark antiquity
Hath flowed, "with pomp of waters unwith-
    stood,"
Roused though it be full often to a mood
Which spurns the check of salutary bands,
That this most famous stream in bogs and sands
Should perish; and to evil and to good
Be lost for ever. In our halls is hung
Armoury of the invincible knights of old;
We must be free or die, who speak the tongue
That Shakespeare spake: the faith and morals
    hold
Which Milton held. In every thing we are
    sprung
Of earth's first blood, have titles manifold.

THE REVERIE OF POOR SUSAN

At the corner of Wood Street, when daylight
    appears,
Hangs a thrush that sings loud, it has sung for
    three years:
Poor Susan has passed by the spot, and has
    heard
In the silence of morning the song of the
    bird.

'Tis a note of enchantment; what ails her?
    She sees
A mountain ascending, a vision of trees;
Bright volumes of vapour through Lothbury
    glide,
And a river flows on through the vale of
    Cheapside.

Green pastures she views in the midst of the
    dale,
Down which she so often has tripped with her
    pail;
And a single small cottage, a nest like a
    dove's,
The one only dwelling on earth that she
    loves.

She looks, and her heart is in heaven: but they
  fade,
The mist and the river, the hill and the
  shade:
The stream will not flow, and the hill will not
  rise,
And the colours have all passed away from her
  eyes.

WRITTEN IN LONDON, SEPTEMBER, 1802

O Friend! I know not which way I must look
For comfort, being, as I am, opprest,
To think that now our life is only drest
For show; mean handy-work of craftsman,
  cook,
Or groom!—We must run glittering like a
  brook
In the open sunshine, or we are unblest:
The wealthiest man among us is the best;
No grandeur now in nature or in book
Delights us. Rapine, avarice, expense,
This is idolatry; and these we adore;
Plain living and high thinking are no more;
The homely beauty of the good old cause
Is gone; our peace, our fearful innocence
And pure religion breathing household laws.

SNOWDON

                With forehead bent
Earthward, as if in opposition set
Against an enemy, I panted up
With eager pace, and no less eager thoughts.
Thus might we wear a midnight hour away,
Ascending at loose distance each from each,
And I, as chanced, the foremost of the band;
When at my feet the ground appeared to
    brighten,
And with a step or two seemed brighter still;
Nor was time given to ask or learn the cause,
For instantly a light upon the turf
Fell like a flash, and lo! as I looked up
The Moon hung naked in a firmament
Of azure without cloud, and at my feet
Rested a silent sea of hoary mist.
A hundred hills their dusky backs upheaved
All over this still ocean; and beyond,
Far, far beyond, the solid vapours stretched,
In headlands, tongues, and promontory shapes,
Into the main Atlantic, that appeared
To dwindle, and give up his majesty,
Usurped upon far as the sight could reach.
Not so the ethereal vault; encroachment none
Was there, nor loss; only the inferior stars

Had disappeared, or shed a fainter light
In the clear presence of the full-orbed Moon,
Who, from her sovereign elevation, gazed
Upon the billowy ocean, as it lay
All meek and silent, save that through a rift—
Not distant from the shore whereon we stood,
A fixed, abysmal, gloomy, breathing-place—
Mounted the roar of waters, torrents, streams
Innumerable, roaring with one voice!
Heard over earth and sea, and, in that hour,
For so it seemed, felt by the starry heavens.

from The Prelude, *Book* 14

LINES WRITTEN IN EARLY SPRING

I heard a thousand blended notes,
While in a grove I sate reclined,
In that sweet mood when pleasant thoughts
Bring sad thoughts to the mind.

To her fair works did nature link
The human soul that through me ran;
And much it grieved my heart to think
What man has made of man.

(a fragment)

AFTER-THOUGHT

I thought of thee, my partner and my guide,
As being past away. Vain sympathies!
For, backward, Duddon! as I cast my eyes,
I see what was, and is, and will abide;
Still glides the stream, and shall for ever glide;
The form remains, the function never dies;
While we, the brave, the mighty, and the wise,
We men, who in our morn of youth defied
The elements, must vanish;—be it so!
Enough, if something from our hands have
   power
To live, and act, and serve the future hour;
And if, as toward the silent tomb we go,
Through love, through hope, and faith's trans-
    cendent dower,
We feel that we are greater than we know.

FRENCH REVOLUTION

Oh! pleasant exercise of hope and joy!
For mighty were the auxiliars, which then stood
Upon our side, we who were strong in love!
Bliss was it in that dawn to be alive,
But to be young was very heaven!—Oh! times,
In which the meagre, stale, forbidding ways
Of custom, law, and statute, took at once
The attraction of a country in romance!
When reason seemed the most to assert her
    rights,
When most intent on making of herself
A prime enchantress—to assist the work,
Which then was going forward in her name!
Not favoured spots alone, but the whole earth,
The beauty wore of promise—that which sets
(As at some moment might not be unfelt
Among the bowers of paradise itself)
The budding rose above the rose full blown.
What temper at the prospect did not wake
To happiness unthought of? The inert
Were roused, and lively natures rapt away!
They who have fed their childhood upon
    dreams,
The playfellows of fancy, who had made
All powers of swiftness, subtilty, and strength

95

Their ministers,—who in lordly wise had
    stirred
Among the grandest objects of the sense,
And dealt with whatsoever they found there
As if they had within some lurking right
To wield it;—they, too, who of gentle mood
Had watched all gentle motions, and to these
Had fitted their own thoughts, schemers more
    mild,
And in the region of their peaceful selves;—
Now was it that both found, the meek and lofty
Did both find helpers to their heart's desire,
And stuff at hand, plastic as they could wish, —
Were called upon to exercise their skill,
Not in Utopia,—subterranean fields,
Or some secreted island, Heaven knows where!
But in the very world, which is the world
Of all of us,—the place where in the end
We find our happiness, or not at all!

SONNET

If thou indeed derive thy light from Heaven,
Then, to the measure of that heaven-born light,
Shine, poet! in thy place, and be content:—
The stars pre-eminent in magnitude,
And they that from the zenith dart their beams,
(Visible though they be to half the earth,
Though half a sphere be conscious of their
    brightness)
Are yet of no diviner origin,
No purer essence, than the one that burns,
Like an untended watch-fire, on the ridge
Of some dark mountain; or than those which
    seem
Humbly to hang, like twinkling winter lamps,
Among the branches of the leafless trees;
All are the undying offspring of one sire:
Then, to the measure of the light vouchsafed,
Shine, poet! in thy place, and be content.

SONG FOR THE SPINNING WHEEL

Swiftly turn the murmuring wheel!
Night has brought the welcome hour,
When the weary fingers feel
Help, as if from faëry power;
Dewy night o'ershades the ground;
Turn the swift wheel round and round!

Now, beneath the starry sky,
Crouch the widely-scattered sheep;—
Ply the pleasant labour, ply!
For the spindle, while they sleep,
Runs with speed more smooth and fine,
Gathering up a trustier line.

Short-lived likings may be bred
By a glance from fickle eyes;
But true love is like the thread
Which the kindly wool supplies,
When the flocks are all at rest
Sleeping on the mountain's breast.

THE POET

He is retired as noontide dew,
Or fountain in a noon-day grove;
And you must love him, ere to you
He will seem worthy of your love.

The outward shows of sky and earth,
Of hill and valley he has viewed;
And impulses of deeper birth
Have come to him in solitude.

In common things that round us lie
Some random truths he can impart,
The harvest of a quiet eye
That broods and sleeps on his own heart.

But he is weak, both man and boy,
Hath been an idler in the land ;
Contented if he might enjoy
The things which others understand.

Come hither in thy hour of strength;
Come, weak as is a braking wave!
Here stretch thy body at full length;
Or build thy house upon this grave:

from A Poet's Epitaph

SONNET

Fair prime of life! were it enough to gild
With ready sunbeams every straggling shower;
And, if an unexpected cloud should lower,
Swiftly thereon a rainbow arch to build
For fancy's errands,—then, from fields half-
    tilled
Gathering green weeds to mix with poppy
    flower,
Thee might thy minions crown, and chant thy
    power,
Unpitied by the wise, all censure stilled.
Ah! show that worthier honours are thy due;
Fair prime of life! arouse the deeper heart;
Confirm the spirit glorying to pursue
Some path of steep ascent and lofty aim;
And, if there be a joy that slights the claim
Of grateful memory, bid that joy depart.

ELEGIAC STANZAS

*Suggested by a picture of Peele Castle, in a storm,
Painted by Sir George Beaumont*

I was thy neighbour once, thou rugged Pile!
Four summer weeks I dwelt in sight of thee:
I saw thee every day; and all the while
Thy Form was sleeping on a glassy sea.

So pure the sky, so quiet was the air!
So like, so very like, was day to day!
Whene'er I looked, thy Image still was there;
It trembled, but it never passed away.

How perfect was the calm! it seemed no sleep;
No mood, which season takes away, or brings:
I could have fancied that the mighty Deep
Was even the gentlest of all gentle Things.

Ah! then, if mine had been the Painter's hand,
To express what then I saw; and add the gleam,
The light that never was, on sea or land,
The consecration, and the Poet's dream;

I would have planted thee, thou hoary Pile
Amid a world how different from this!
Beside a sea that could not cease to smile;
On tranquil land, beneath a sky of bliss.

Thou shouldst have seemed a treasure-house
    divine
Of peaceful years; a chronicle of heaven;—
Of all the sunbeams that did ever shine
The very sweetest had to thee been given.

A Picture had it been of lasting ease,
Elysian quiet, without toil or strife;
No motion but the moving tide, a breeze,
Or merely silent Nature's breathing life.

Such, in the fond illusion of my heart,
Such Picture would I at that time have
    made:
And seen the soul of truth in every part,
A steadfast peace that might not be betrayed.

So once it would have been,—'tis so no
    more;
I have submitted to a new control:
A power is gone, which nothing can restore;
A deep distress hath humanised my Soul.

Not for a moment could I now behold
A smiling sea, and be what I have been:
The feeling of my loss will ne'er be old;
This, which I know, I speak with mind
    serene.

Then, Beaumont, Friend! Who would have
    been the Friend,
If he had lived, of Him whom I deplore,
This work of thine I blame not, but commend;
This sea in anger, and that dismal shore.

O 'tis a passionate Work!—yet wise and well,
Well chosen is the spirit that is here;
That Hulk which labours in the deadly swell,
This rueful sky, this pageantry of fear!

And this huge Castle, standing here sublime,
I love to see the look with which it braves,
Cased in the unfeeling armour of old time,
The lightning, the fierce wind, and trampling
    waves.

Farewell, farewell the heart that lives alone,
Housed in a dream, at distance from the Kind!
Such happiness, wherever it be known,
Is to be pitied; for 'tis surely blind.

But welcome fortitude, and patient cheer,
And frequent sights of what is to be borne!
Such sights, or worse, as are before me here.—
Not without hope we suffer and we mourn.

TO A SNOWDROP

Lone flower, hemmed in with snows, and white
as they,
But hardier far, once more I see thee bend
Thy forehead, as if fearful to offend,
Like an unbidden guest. Though day by day,
Storms, sallying from the mountain-tops, way-
lay
The rising sun, and on the plains descend;
Yet art thou welcome, welcome as a friend
Whose zeal outruns his promise! Blue-eyed
May
Shall soon behold this border thickly set
With bright jonquils, their odours lavishing
On the soft west-wind and his frolic peers;
Nor will I then thy modest grace forget,
Chaste snowdrop, venturous harbinger of
spring,
And pensive monitor of fleeting years!

REMEMBRANCE

When, in the blessèd hours
Of early love, the loved one at my side
I roamed, in daily presence of this scene,
Upon the naked pool and dreary crags,
And on the melancholy beacon, fell
A spirit of pleasure and youth's golden gleam;
And think ye not with radiance more sublime
For these remembrances, and for the power
They had left behind? So feeling comes in aid
Of feeling, and diversity of strength
Attends us, if but once we have been strong.

from The Prelude, *Book* 12

MUTABILITY

Hast thou seen, with flash incessant,
Bubbles gliding under ice,
Bodied forth and evanescent
No one knows by what device?

Such are thoughts!—A wind-swept meadow
Mimicking a troubled sea,
Such is life; and death a shadow
From the rock eternity!

SONNET: MUTABILITY

From low to high doth dissolution climb,
And sink from high to low, along a scale
Of awful notes, whose concord shall not fail;
A musical but melancholy chime,
Which they can hear who meddle not with
    crime,
Nor avarice, nor over-anxious care.
Truth fails not; but her outward forms that
    bear
The longest date do melt like frosty rime,
That in the morning whitened hill and plain
And is no more; drop like the tower sublime
Of yesterday, which royally did wear
His crown of weeds, but could not even sustain
Some casual shout that broke the silent air,
Or the unimaginable touch of Time.

INFLUENCE OF NATURAL OBJECTS

Wisdom and Spirit of the universe!
Thou soul, that art the eternity of thought!
And giv'st to forms and images a breath
And everlasting motion! not in vain,
By day or star light, thus from my first dawn
Of childhood didst thou intertwine for me
The passions that build up our human soul;
Not with the mean and vulgar works of man,—
But with high objects, with enduring things,
With life and nature; purifying thus
The elements of feeling and of thought,
And sanctifying by such discipline
Both pain and fear,—until we recognise
A grandeur in the beatings of the heart.

  Nor was this fellowship vouchsafed to me
With stinted kindness. In November days,
When vapours rolling down the valleys made
A lonely scene more lonesome; among woods
At noon; and 'mid the calm of summer nights,
When, by the margin of the trembling lake,
Beneath the gloomy hills, homeward I went
In solitude, such intercourse was mine:
Mine was it in the fields both day and night,
And by the waters, all the summer long;

And in the frosty season, when the sun
Was set, and visible for many a mile,
The cottage windows through the twilight
    blazed,
I heeded not the summons:—happy time
It was indeed for all of us; for me
It was a time of rapture!—Clear and loud
The village clock tolled six—I wheeled about,
Proud and exulting like an untired horse
That cares not for his home.—All shod with
    steel
We hissed along the polished ice, in games
Confederate, imitative of the chase
And woodland pleasures,—the resounding horn,
The pack loud-chiming, and the hunted hare.
So through the darkness and the cold we flew,
And not a voice was idle: with the din
Smitten, the precipices rang aloud;
The leafless trees and every icy crag
Tinkled like iron; while far-distant hills
Into the tumult sent an alien sound
Of melancholy, not unnoticed, while the stars,
Eastward, were sparkling clear, and in the west
The orange sky of evening died away.

Not seldom from the uproar I retired
Into a silent bay,—or sportively
Glanced sideway, leaving the tumultuous
    throng,

To cut across the reflex of a star,
Image, that, flying still before me, gleamed
Upon the glassy plain: and oftentimes,
When we had given our bodies to the wind,
And all the shadowy banks on either side
Came sweeping through the darkness, spinning still
The rapid line of motion, then at once
Have I, reclining back upon my heels,
Stopped short; yet still the solitary cliffs
Wheeled by me—even as if the earth had rolled
With visible motion her diurnal round!
Behind me did they stretch in solemn train,
Feebler and feebler, and I stood and watched
Till all was tranquil as a summer sea.

from The Prelude, *Book* 1

NEWTON

By light
Of moon or favouring stars I could behold
The antechapel, where the statue stood
Of Newton with his prism and silent face,
The marble index of a mind for ever
Voyaging through strange seas of Thought, alone.

from The Prelude, *Book* 3

KING'S COLLEGE CHAPEL, CAMBRIDGE

Tax not the royal Saint with vain expense,
With ill-matched aims the Architect who
    planned—
Albeit labouring for a scanty band
Of white-robed Scholars only—this immense
And glorious Work of fine intelligence!
Give all thou canst; high Heaven rejects the
    lore
Of nicely-calculated less or more;
So deemed the man who fashioned for the sense
These lofty pillars, spread that branching roof
Self-poised, and scooped into ten thousand
    cells,
Where light and shade repose, where music
    dwells
Lingering—and wandering on as loath to die;
Like thoughts whose very sweetness yieldeth
    proof
That they were born for immortality.

LINES WRITTEN WHILE SAILING IN A BOAT
AT EVENING

How richly glows the water's breast
Before us, tinged with evening hues,
While, facing thus the crimson west,
The boat her silent course pursues!
And see how dark the backward stream!
A little moment past so smiling!
And still, perhaps, with faithless gleam,
Some other loiterers beguiling.

Such views the youthful Bard allure;
But, heedless of the following gloom,
He deems their colours shall endure
Till peace go with him to the tomb.
—And let him nurse his fond deceit,
And what if he must die in sorrow!
Who would not cherish dreams so sweet,
Though grief and pain may come to-morrow?

SONNET

Nuns fret not at their convent's narrow room:
And hermits are contented with their cells;
And students with their pensive citadels:
Maids at the wheel, the weaver at his loom,
Sit blithe and happy; bees that soar for bloom,
High as the highest peak of Furness Fells,
Will murmur by the hour in foxglove bells:
In truth, the prison, unto which we doom
Ourselves, no prison is: and hence to me,
In sundry moods, 'twas pastime to be bound
Within the sonnet's scanty plot of ground;
Pleased if some souls (for such there needs
    must be)
Who have felt the weight of too much liberty,
Should find brief solace there, as I have found.

YEW-TREES

There is a yew-tree, pride of Lorton Vale,
Which to this day stands single, in the midst
Of its own darkness, as it stood of yore,
Not loath to furnish weapons for the bands
Of Umfraville or Percy ere they marched
To Scotland's heaths; or those that crossed the sea
And drew their sounding bows at Azincour,
Perhaps at earlier Crecy, or Poictiers.
Of vast circumference and gloom profound
This solitary tree!—a living thing
Produced too slowly ever to decay;
Of form and aspect too magnificent
To be destroyed. But worthier still of note
Are those fraternal four of Borrowdale,
Joined in one solemn and capacious grove;
Huge trunks!—and each particular trunk a
      growth
Of intertwisted fibres serpentine
Up-coiling, and inveterately convolved,—
Nor uninformed with phantasy, and looks
That threaten the profane;—a pillared shade,
Upon whose grassless floor of red-brown hue,
By sheddings from the pining umbrage tinged
Perennially—beneath whose sable roof
Of boughs, as if for festal purpose decked

With unrejoicing berries, ghostly shapes
May meet at noontide—Fear and trembling
    Hope,
Silence and Foresight—Death the Skeleton,
And Time the Shadow,—there to celebrate,
As in a natural temple scattered o'er
With altars undisturbed of mossy stone,
United worship; or in mute repose
To lie, and listen to the mountain flood
Murmuring from Glaramara's inmost caves.

SEPTEMBER, 1802. NEAR DOVER

Inland, within a hollow vale, I stood;
And saw, while sea was calm and air was clear,
The coast of France, the coast of France how
    near!
Drawn almost into frightful neighbourhood.
I shrunk, for verily the barrier flood
Was like a lake, or river bright and fair,
A span of waters; yet what power is there!
What mightiness for evil and for good!
Even so doth God protect us if we be
Virtuous and wise. Winds blow, and waters roll,
Strength to the brave, and power, and deity,
Yet in themselves are nothing! One decree
Spake laws to *them*, and said that by the soul
Only the nations shall be great and free!

THE SOLITARY

So was he lifted gently from the ground,
And with their freight homeward the shepherds
    moved
Through the dull mist, I following—when a step,
A single step, that freed me from the skirts
Of the blind vapour, opened to my view
Glory beyond all glory ever seen
By waking sense or by the dreaming soul!
The appearance, instantaneously disclosed,
Was of a mighty city—boldly say
A wilderness of building, sinking far
And self-withdrawn into a boundless depth,
Far sinking into splendour—without end!
Fabric it seemed of diamond and of gold,
With alabaster domes, and silver spires,
And blazing terrace upon terrace, high
Uplifted; here, serene pavilions bright,
In avenues disposed; there, towers begirt
With battlements that on their restless fronts
Bore stars—illumination of all gems!
By earthly nature had the effect been wrought
Upon the dark materials of the storm
Now pacified; on them, and on the coves
And mountain-steeps and summits, whereunto
The vapours had receded, taking there
Their station under a cerulean sky.

Oh, 'twas an unimaginable sight!
Clouds, mists, streams, watery rocks and
    emerald turf,
Clouds of all tincture, rocks and sapphire sky,
Confused, commingled, mutually inflamed,
Molten together, and composing thus,
Each lost in each, that marvellous array
Of temple, palace, citadel, and huge
Fantastic pomp of structure without name,
In fleecy folds voluminous, enwrapped.
Right in the midst, where interspace appeared
Of open court, an object like a throne
Under a shining canopy of state
Stood fixed; and fixed resemblances were seen
To implements of ordinary use,
But vast in size, in substance glorified;
Such as by Hebrew Prophets were beheld
In vision—forms uncouth of mightiest power
For admiration and mysterious awe.
This little Vale, a dwelling-place of Man,
Lay low beneath my feet; 'twas visible—
I saw not, but I felt that it was there.
That which I *saw* was the revealed abode
Of Spirits in beatitude: my heart
Swelled in my breast—"I have been dead," I
    cried,
"And now I live! Oh! wherefore *do* I live?"
And with that pang I prayed to be no more!

from The Excursion, *Book* 2

SONNET

Pelion and Ossa flourish side by side,
Together in immortal books enrolled:
His ancient dower Olympus hath not sold;
And that inspiring hill which "did divide
Into two ample horns his forehead wide,"
Shines with poetic radiance as of old;
While not an English mountain we behold
By the celestial muses glorified.
Yet round our sea-girt shore they rise in
    crowds:
What was the great Parnassus' self to thee,
Mount Skiddaw? In his natural sovereignty
Our British hill is nobler far: he shrouds
His double front among Atlantic clouds,
And pours forth streams more sweet than
    Castaly.

WATER-FOWL

Mark how the feathered tenants of the flood,
With grace of motion that might scarcely seem
Inferior to angelical, prolong
Their curious pastime! shaping in mid air
(And sometimes with ambitious wing that
    soars
High as the level of the mountain tops)
A circuit ampler than the lake beneath,
Their own domain;—but ever, while intent
On tracing and retracing that large round,
Their jubilant activity evolves
Hundreds of curves and circles, to and fro,
Upward and downward, progress intricate,
Yet unperplexed, as if one spirit swayed
Their indefatigable flight.—'Tis done—
Ten times, or more, I fancied it had ceased;
But lo! the vanished company again
Ascending;—they approach—I hear their wings
Faint, faint at first; and then an eager sound
Past in a moment—and as faint again!
They tempt the sun to sport amid their plumes;
They tempt the water, or the gleaming ice,
To show them a fair image;—'tis themselves,
Their own fair forms, upon the glimmering
    plain,

Painted more soft and fair as they descend
Almost to touch;—then up again aloft,
Up with a sally and a flash of speed,
As if they scorned both resting-place and rest!

SONNET

Scorn not the sonnet; critic, you have frowned,
Mindless of its just honours;—with this key
Shakespeare unlocked his heart; the melody
Of this small lute gave ease to Petrarch's
　　wound;
A thousand times this pipe did Tasso sound;
With it Camöens soothed an exile's grief;
The sonnet glittered a gay myrtle leaf
Amid the cypress with which Dante crowned
His visionary brow: a glow-worm lamp,
It cheered mild Spenser, called from faery land
To struggle through dark ways; and when a
　　damp
Fell round the path of Milton, in his hand
The thing became a trumpet, whence he blew
Soul-animating strains—alas, too few!

ADDRESS TO KILCHURN CASTLE, UPON LOCH AWE

Child of loud-throated war! the mountain
    stream
Roars in thy hearing; but thy hour of rest
Is come, and thou art silent in thy age;
Save when the wind sweeps by and sounds are
    caught
Ambiguous, neither wholly thine nor theirs.
Oh! there is life that breathes not: powers there
    are
That touch each other to the quick in modes
Which the gross world no sense hath to
    perceive,
No soul to dream of. What art thou, from care
Cast off—abandoned by thy rugged sire,
Nor by soft peace adopted; though, in place
And in dimension, such that thou mightest
    seem
But a mere footstool to yon sovereign lord,
Huge Cruachan, (a thing that meaner hills
Might crush, nor know that it had suffered
    harm;)
Yet he, not loth, in favour of thy claims
To reverence suspends his own; submitting
All that the God of nature hath conferred,

All that he holds in common with the stars,
To the memorial majesty of time
Impersonated in thy calm decay!
Take, then, thy seat, vicegerent unreproved!
Now, while a farewell gleam of evening light
Is fondly lingering on thy shattered front,
Do thou, in turn, be paramount; and rule
Over the pomp and beauty of a scene
Whose mountains, torrents, lake, and woods,
    unite
To pay thee homage; and with these are joined,
In willing admiration and respect,
Two hearts, which in thy presence might be
    called
Youthful as spring. Shade of departed power.
Skeleton of unfleshed humanity,
The chronicle were welcome that should call
Into the compass of distinct regard
The toils and struggles of thy infant years!
Yon foaming flood seems motionless as ice,
Its dizzy turbulence eludes the eye,
Frozen by distance: so, majestic pile,
To the perception of this age, appear
Thy fierce beginnings, softened and subdued
And quieted in character; the strife,
The pride, the fury uncontrollable,
Lost on the aërial heights of the Crusades! [1]

[1] The tradition is that the castle was built by a lady during the
absence of her lord in Palestine.

CALAIS, AUGUST, 1802

Is it a reed that's shaken by the wind,
Or what is it that ye go forth to see?
Lords, lawyers, statesmen, squires of low degree,
Men known, and men unknown, sick, lame, and
    blind,
Post forward all, like creatures of one kind,
With first-fruit offerings crowd to bend the
    knee
In France, before the new-born majesty.
'Tis ever thus. Ye men of prostrate mind!
A seemly reverence may be paid to power;
But that's a loyal virtue, never sown
In haste, nor springing with a transient shower
When truth, when sense, when liberty were
    flown,
What hardship had it been to wait an hour?
Shame on you, feeble heads, to slavery prone!

THE SIMPLON PASS

                              Brook and road
Were fellow-travellers in this gloomy Pass,
And with them did we journey several hours
At a slow step. The immeasurable height
Of woods decaying, never to be decayed,
The stationary blasts of waterfalls,
And in the narrow rent, at every turn,
Winds thwarting winds bewildered and forlorn,
The torrents shooting from the clear blue sky,
The rocks that muttered close upon our ears,
Black drizzling crags that spake by the wayside
As if a voice were in them, the sick sight
And giddy prospect of the raving stream,
The unfettered clouds and region of the
     heavens,
Tumult and peace, the darkness and the light—
Were all like workings of one mind, the features
Of the same face, blossoms upon one tree,
Characters of the great Apocalypse,
The types and symbols of Eternity;
Of first, and last, and midst, and without end.

from The Prelude, *Book* 4

THE RIVER DUDDON

Return, content! for fondly I pursued,
Even when a child, the streams—unheard,
     unseen;
Through tangled woods, impending rocks
     between;
Or, free as air, with flying inquest viewed
The sullen reservoirs whence their bold brood,
Pure as the morning, fretful, boisterous, keen,
Green as the salt-sea billows, white and green,
Poured down the hills, a choral multitude!
Nor have I tracked their course for scanty gains;
They taught me random cares and truant joys,
That shield from mischief and preserve from
     stains
Vague minds, while men are growing out of
     boys;
Maturer fancy owes to their rough noise
Impetuous thoughts that brook not servile
     reins.

A NIGHT THOUGHT

Lo! where the Moon along the sky
Sails with her happy destiny;
Oft is she hid from mortal eye
    Or dimly seen,
But when the clouds asunder fly
    How bright her mien!

Far different we—a froward race,
Thousands though rich in Fortune's grace
With cherished sullenness of pace
    Their way pursue,
Ingrates who wear a smileless face
    The whole year through.

If kindred humours e'er would make
My spirit droop for drooping's sake,
From Fancy following in thy wake,
    Bright ship of heaven!
A counter impulse let me take
    And be forgiven.

SONNET

With ships the sea was sprinkled far and nigh,
Like stars in heaven, and joyously it showed;
Some lying fast at anchor in the road,
Some veering up and down, one knew not why.
A goodly vessel did I then espy
Come like a giant from a haven broad;
And lustily along the bay she strode,
Her tackling rich, and of apparel high,
This ship was naught to me, nor I to her,
Yet I pursued her with a lover's look;
This ship to all the rest did I prefer:
When will she turn, and whither? She will
    brook
No tarrying; where she comes the winds must
    stir:
On went she,—and due north her journey took.

SHADOW AND SUBSTANCE

As one who hangs down-bending from the
    side
Of a slow-moving boat, upon the breast
Of a still water, solacing himself
With such discoveries as his eye can make
Beneath him in the bottom of the deep,
Sees many beauteous sights—weeds, fishes,
    flowers,
Grots, pebbles, roots of trees, and fancies more,
Yet often is perplexed and cannot part
The shadow from the substance, rocks and sky,
Mountains and clouds, reflected in the depth
Of the clear flood, from things which there
    abide
In their true dwelling; now is crossed by gleam
Of his own image, by a sunbeam now,
And wavering motions sent he knows not
    whence,
Impediments that make his task more sweet;
Such pleasant office have we long pursued
Incumbent o'er the surface of past time.

from The Prelude, *Book* 4

SONNET

Where lies the land to which yon ship must go?
Fresh as a lark mounting at break of day,
Festively she puts forth in trim array;
Is she for tropic suns, or polar snow?
What boots the inquiry?—Neither friend nor
    foe
She cares for; let her travel where she may,
She finds familiar names, a beaten way
Ever before her, and a wind to blow.
Yet still I ask, what haven is her mark?
And, almost as it was when ships were rare,
(From time to time, like pilgrims, here and
    there
Crossing the waters) doubt, and something
    dark,
Of the old sea some reverential fear,
Is with me at thy farewell, joyous bark!

AIREY-FORCE VALLEY

Not a breath of air
Ruffles the bosom of this leafy glen.
From the brook's margin, wide around, the
trees
Are steadfast as the rocks; the brook itself,
Old as the hills that feed it from afar,
Doth rather deepen than disturb the calm
Where all things else are still and motionless.
And yet, even now, a little breeze perchance
Escaped from boisterous winds that rage
without,
Has entered, by the sturdy oaks unfelt,
But to its gentle touch how sensitive
Is the light ash! that, pendent from the brow
Of yon dim cave, in seeming silence makes
A soft eye-music of slow-waving boughs,
Powerful almost as vocal harmony
To stay the wanderer's steps and soothe his
thoughts.

A SUMMER'S EVENING

One summer evening (led by her) I found
A little boat tied to a willow tree
Within a rocky cave, its usual home.
Straight I unloosed her chain, and stepping in
Pushed from the shore. It was an act of stealth
And troubled pleasure, nor without the voice
Of mountain-echoes did my boat move on;
Leaving behind her still, on either side,
Small circles glittering idly in the moon,
Until they melted all into one track
Of sparkling light. But now, like one who rows,
Proud of his skill, to reach a chosen point
With an unswerving line, I fixed my view
Upon the summit of a craggy ridge,
The horizon's utmost boundary; far above
Was nothing but the stars and the grey sky.
She was an elfin pinnace; lustily
I dipped my oars into the silent lake,
And, as I rose upon the stroke, my boat
Went heaving through the water like a swan;
When, from behind that craggy steep till then
The horizon's bound, a huge peak, black and
    huge,
As if with voluntary power instinct
Upreared its head. I struck and struck again,

And growing still in stature the grim shape
Towered up between me and the stars, and still,
For so it seemed, with purpose of its own
And measured motion like a living thing,
Strode after me. With trembling oars I turned,
And through the silent water stole my way
Back to the covert of the willow tree:
There in her mooring-place I left my bark,—
And through the meadows homeward went, in grave
And serious mood; but after I had seen
That spectacle, for many days, my brain
Worked with a dim and undetermined sense
Of unknown modes of being; o'er my thoughts
There hung a darkness, call it solitude
Or blank desertion. No familiar shapes
Remained, no pleasant images of trees,
Of sea or sky, no colours of green fields;
But huge and mighty forms, that do not live
Like living men, moved slowly through the mind
By day, and were a trouble to my dreams.

from The Prelude, *Book* 1

ECHO UPON THE GEMMI

What beast of chase hath broken from the
    cover?
Stern Gemmi listens to as full a cry,
As multitudinous a harmony,
Of sounds as rang the heights of Latmos over,
When, from the soft couch of her sleeping lover,
Up-starting, Cynthia skimmed the mountain-
    dew
In keen pursuit—and gave, where'er she flew,
Impetuous motion to the stars above her.
A solitary wolf-dog, ranging on
Through the bleak concave, wakes this
    wondrous chime
Of aëry voices locked in unison,—
Faint—far-off—near—deep—solemn and sub-
    lime!
So, from the body of one guilty deed,
A thousand ghostly fears, and haunting
    thoughts, proceed!

CHARACTERISTICS OF A CHILD THREE YEARS OLD

Loving she is, and tractable, though wild;
And innocence hath privilege in her
To dignify arch looks and laughing eyes;
And feats of cunning; and the pretty round
Of trespasses, affected to provoke
Mock-chastisement and partnership in play.
And, as a faggot sparkles on the hearth,
Not less if unattended and alone
Than when both young and old sit gathered
    round
And take delight in its activity,
Even so this happy creature of herself
Is all-sufficient; solitude to her
Is blithe society who fills the air
With gladness and involuntary songs,
Light are her sallies as the tripping fawn's
Forth-startled from the fern where she lay
    couched;
Unthought of, unexpected, as the stir
Of the soft breeze ruffling the meadow
    flowers;
Or from before it chasing wantonly
The many-coloured images impressed
Upon the bosom of a placid lake.

COMPOSED BY THE SIDE OF GRASMERE
LAKE, 1807

Clouds, lingering yet, extend in solid bars
Through the gray west; and lo! these waters,
    steeled
By breezeless air to smoothest polish, yield
A vivid repetition of the stars;
Jove—Venus—and the ruddy crest of Mars,
Amid his fellows beauteously revealed
At happy distance from earth's groaning field,
Where ruthless mortals wage incessant wars.
Is it a mirror?—or the nether sphere
Opening to view the abyss in which she feeds
Her own calm fires?—But list! a voice is near;
Great Pan himself low-whispering through the
    reeds,
"Be thankful, thou; for if unholy deeds
Ravage the world, tranquillity is here!"

TO M. H.

Our walk was far among the ancient trees;
There was no road, nor any woodman's path;
But a thick umbrage, checking the wild growth
Of weed and sapling, along soft green turf
Beneath the branches, of itself had made
A track, that brought us to a slip of lawn,
And a small bed of water in the woods.
All round this pool both flocks and herds might
    drink
On its firm margin, even as from a well,
Or some stone-basin which the herdsman's hand
Had shaped for their refreshment; nor did sun
Or wind from any quarter, ever come,
But as a blessing, to this calm recess,
This glade of water and this one green field.
The spot was made by nature for herself,
The travellers know it not, and 'twill remain
Unknown to them: but it is beautiful;
And if a man should plant his cottage near,
Should sleep beneath the shelter of its trees,
And blend its waters with his daily meal,
He would so love it, that in his death hour
Its image would survive among his thoughts;
And therefore, my sweet Mary, this still nook,
With all its beeches, we have named from you.

THE WILD DUCK'S NEST

The imperial consort of the fairy king
Owns not a sylvan bower; or gorgeous cell
With emerald floored, and with purpureal shell
Ceilinged and roofed, that is so fair a thing
As this low structure—for the tasks of spring
Prepared by one who loves the buoyant swell
Of the brisk waves, yet here consents to dwell;
And spreads in steadfast peace her brooding-
    wing.
Words cannot paint the o'ershadowing yew-
    tree-bough,
And dimly-gleaming nest,—a hollow crown
Of golden leaves inlaid with silver down,
Fine as the mother's softest plumes allow;
I gazed—and, self-accused while gazing, sighed
For human-kind, weak slaves of cumbrous
    pride!

GLEN-ALMAIN, OR THE NARROW GLEN

In this still place, remote from men,
Sleeps Ossian, in the Narrow glen;
In this still place, where murmurs on
But one meek streamlet, only one:
He sang of battles, and the breath
Of stormy war, and violent death;
And should, methinks, when all was past,
Have rightfully been laid at last
Where rocks were rudely heaped, and rent
As by a spirit turbulent;
Where sights were rough, and sounds were wild
And every thing unreconciled;
In some complaining, dim retreat,
For fear and melancholy meet;
But this is calm; there cannot be
A more entire tranquillity.

Does then the bard sleep here indeed?
Or is it but a groundless creed!
What matters it?—I blame them not
Whose fancy in this lonely spot
Was moved; and in such way expressed
Their notion of its perfect rest.
A convent, even a hermit's cell
Would break the silence of this dell:

It is not quiet; is not ease;
But something deeper far than these:
The separation that is here
Is of the grave; and of austere
Yet happy feelings of the dead:
And, therefore, was it rightly said
That Ossian, last of all his race!
Lies buried in this lonely place.

O NIGHTINGALE! THOU SURELY ART

O Nightingale! thou surely art
A creature of a fiery heart:—
These notes of thine—they pierce and pierce;
Tumultuous harmony and fierce!
Thou sing'st as if the god of wine
Had helped thee to a valentine;
A song in mockery and despite
Of shades, and dews, and silent night;
And steady bliss, and all the loves
Now sleeping in these peaceful groves.

(a fragment)

138

SONNET: TO THE CUCKOO

Not the whole warbling grove in concert heard
When sunshine follows shower, the breast can
    thrill
Like the first summons, cuckoo! of thy bill,
With its twin notes inseparably paired.
The captive, 'mid damp vaults unsunned, un-
    aired,
Measuring the periods of his lonely doom,
That cry can reach; and to the sick man's room
Sends gladness, by no languid smile declared,
The lordly eagle-race through hostile search
May perish; time may come when never more
The wilderness shall hear the lion roar;
But long as cock shall crow from household
    perch
To rouse the dawn, soft gales shall speed thy
    wing,
And thy erratic voice be faithful to the spring!

TO THE CUCKOO

O blithe new-comer! I have heard,
I hear thee and rejoice.
O Cuckoo! shall I call thee bird,
Or but a wandering voice?

While I am lying on the grass
Thy twofold shout I hear,
From hill to hill it seems to pass,
At once far off and near.

Though babbling only, to the vale,
Of sunshine and of flowers,
Thou bringest unto me a tale
Of visionary hours.

Thrice welcome, darling of the spring!
Even yet thou art to me
No bird: but an invisible thing,
A voice, a mystery.

The same whom in my school-boy days
I listened to; that cry
Which made me look a thousand ways
In bush, and tree, and sky.

To seek thee did I often rove
Through woods and on the green;
And thou wert still a hope, a love;
Still longed for, never seen.

And I can listen to thee yet;
Can lie upon the plain
And listen, till I do beget
That golden time again.

O blessed bird! the earth we pace
Again appears to be
An unsubstantial faery place;
That is fit home for thee!

SONNET

There is a little unpretending rill
Of limpid water, humbler far than aught
That ever among men or naiads sought
Notice or name!—It quivers down the hill,
Furrowing its shallow way with dubious will;
Yet to my mind this scanty stream is brought
Oftener than Ganges or the Nile, a thought
Of private recollection sweet and still!
Months perish with their moons; year treads
    on year;
But, faithful Emma, thou with me canst say
That, while ten thousand pleasures disappear,
And flies their memory fast almost as they,
The immortal spirit of one happy day
Lingers beside that rill, in vision clear.

ODE TO DUTY

"Jam non consilio bonus, sed more eò perductus, ut non tantum rectè facere possim, sed nisi rectè facere non possim."

Stern daughter of the voice of God!
O Duty! if that name thou love,
Who art a light to guide, a rod
To check the erring, and reprove;
Thou who art victory and law
When empty terrors overawe;
From vain temptations dost set free;
And calm'st the weary strife of frail humanity!

There are who ask not if thine eye
Be on them; who, in love and truth,
Where no misgiving is, rely
Upon the genial sense of youth;
Glad hearts! without reproach or blot;
Who do thy work, and know it not:
Oh! if through confidence misplaced
They fail, thy saving arms, dread Power!
    around them cast.

Serene will be our days and bright,
And happy will our nature be,
When love is an unerring light,
And joy its own security.

And they a blissful course may hold
Even now, who, not unwisely bold,:
Live in the spirit of this creed;
Yet seek thy firm support, according to their
    need.

I, loving freedom, and untried;
No sport of every random gust,
Yet being to myself a guide,
Too blindly have reposed my trust:
And oft, when in my heart was heard
Thy timely mandate, I deferred
The task, in smoother walks to stray;
But thee I now would serve more strictly, if I
    may.

Through no disturbance of my soul,
Or strong compunction in me wrought,
I supplicate for thy control;
But in the quietness of thought:
Me this unchartered freedom tires;
I feel the weight of chance-desires:
My hopes no more must change their name,
I long for a repose that ever is the same.

Stern lawgiver! yet thou dost wear
The Godhead's most benignant grace;
Nor know we anything so fair
As is the smile upon thy face:

Flowers laugh before thee on their beds;
And fragrance in thy footing treads;
Thou dost preserve the stars from wrong;
And the most ancient heavens, through thee,
    are fresh and strong.

To humbler functions, awful power!
I call thee: I myself commend
Unto thy guidance from this hour;
Oh, let my weakness have an end!
Give unto me, made lowly wise,
The spirit of self-sacrifice;
The confidence of reason give;
And in the light of truth thy bondman let me
    live!

A WOMAN'S FEARS

My apprehensions come in crowds;
I dread the rustling of the grass;
The very shadows of the clouds
Have power to shake me as they pass:
I question things and do not find
One that will answer to my mind;
And all the world appears unkind.

from The Affliction of Margaret

TO A SKYLARK

Ethereal minstrel! pilgrim of the sky!
Dost thou despise the earth where cares
    abound?
Or, while the wings aspire, are heart and eye
Both with thy nest upon the dewy ground?
Thy nest which thou canst drop into at will,
Those quivering wings composed, that music
    still!

Leave to the nightingale her shady wood;
A privacy of glorious light is thine;
Whence thou dost pour upon the world a flood
Of harmony, with instinct more divine;
Type of the wise who soar, but never roam;
True to the kindred points of heaven and home!

TO ——,

On Her First Ascent to the Summit of Helvellyn

Inmate of a mountain-dwelling,
Thou has clomb aloft, and gazed,
From the watch-towers of Helvellyn;
Awed, delighted, and amazed!

Potent was the spell that bound thee,
Not unwilling to obey;
For blue ether's arms, flung round thee,
Stilled the pantings of dismay.

Lo! the dwindled woods and meadows!
What a vast abyss is there!
Lo! the clouds, the solemn shadows,
And the glistenings—heavenly fair!

And a record of commotion
Which a thousand ridges yield;
Ridge, and gulf, and distant ocean
Gleaming like a silver shield!

Maiden! now take flight;—inherit
Alps or Andes—they are thine!
With the morning's roseate spirit,
Sweep their length of snowy line;

Or survey their bright dominions
In the gorgeous colours drest,
Flung from off the purple pinions,
Evening spreads throughout the west!

Thine are all the choral fountains
Warbling in each sparry vault
Of the untrodden lunar mountains;
Listen to their songs!—or halt,

To Niphates top invited,
Whither spiteful Satan steered;
Or descend where the ark alighted,
When the green earth re-appeared;

For the power of hills is on thee,
As was witnessed through thine eye
Then, when old Helvellyn won thee
To confess their majesty!

TO TOUSSAINT L'OUVERTURE

Toussaint, the most unhappy man of men!
  Whether the whistling rustic tend his plough
Within thy hearing, or thy head be now
Pillowed in some deep dungeon's earless den;
O miserable chieftain! where and when
Wilt thou find patience? Yet die not! do thou
Wear rather in thy bonds a cheerful brow:
Though fallen thyself never to rise again,
Live, and take comfort. Thou hast left behind
Powers that will work for thee, air, earth, and
    skies:
There's not a breathing of the common wind
That will forget thee; thou hast great allies;
Thy friends are exultations, agonies,
And love, and man's unconquerable mind.

THE DANISH BOY [1]

A Fragment

Between two sister moorland rills
There is a spot that seems to lie
Sacred to flowerets of the hills,
And sacred to the sky.
And in this smooth and open dell
There is a tempest-stricken tree;
A corner-stone by lightning cut,
The last stone of a lonely hut;
And in this dell you see
A thing no storm can e'er destroy,
The shadow of a Danish boy.

In clouds above, the lark is heard,
But drops not here to earth for rest:
Within this lonesome nook the bird
Did never build her nest.
No beast, no bird hath here his home;
Bees, wafted on the breezy air,

---

[1] These stanzas were designed to introduce a ballad upon the story of a Danish prince who had fled from battle, and for the sake of the valuables about him, was murdered by the inhabitant of a cottage in which he had taken refuge. The house fell under a curse, and the spirit of the youth, it was believed, haunted the valley where the crime had been committed.

Pass high above those fragrant bells
To other flowers; to other dells
Their burthens do they bear;
The Danish boy walks here alone:
The lovely dell is all his own.

A spirit of noon-day is he;
Yet seems a form of flesh and blood;
Nor piping shepherd shall he be
Nor herd-boy of the wood.
A regal vest of fur he wears,
In colour like a raven's wing;
It fears not rain, nor wind, nor dew;
But in the storm 'tis fresh and blue
As budding pines in spring;
His helmet has a vernal grace,
Fresh as the bloom upon his face.

A harp is from his shoulder slung;
Resting the harp upon his knee;
To words of a forgotten tongue,
He suits its melody.
Of flocks upon the neighbouring hill
He is the darling and the joy;
And often, when no cause appears,
The mountain ponies prick their ears,
They hear the Danish boy,
While in the dell he sits alone
Beside the tree and corner-stone.

There sits he: in his face you spy
No trace of a ferocious air,
Nor ever was a cloudless sky
So steady or so fair.
The lovely Danish boy is blest
And happy in his flowery cove:
From bloody deeds his thoughts are far,
And yet he warbles songs of war,
That seem like songs of love,
For calm and gentle is his mien;
Like a dead boy he is serene.

TO R. B. HAYDON

High is our calling, friend!—Creative art
(Whether the instrument of words she use,
Or pencil pregnant with ethereal hues,)
Demands the service of a mind and heart,
Though sensitive, yet, in their weakest part,
Heroically fashioned—to infuse
Faith in the whispers of the lonely muse,
While the whole world seems adverse to desert.
And oh! when nature sinks, as oft she may,
Through long-lived pressure of obscure distress,
Still to be strenuous for the bright reward,
And in the soul admit of no decay,
Brook no continuance of weak-mindedness;
Great is the glory, for the strife is hard!

SEPTEMBER, 1819

The sylvan slopes with corn-clad fields
Are hung, as if with golden shields,
Bright trophies of the sun!
Like a fair sister of the sky,
Unruffled doth the blue lake lie,
The mountains looking on.

And, sooth to say, yon vocal grove,
Albeit uninspired by love,
By love untaught to ring,
May well afford to mortal ear
An impulse more profoundly dear
Than music of the spring.

For *that* from turbulence and heat
Proceeds, from some uneasy seat
In nature's struggling frame,
Some region of impatient life;
And jealousy, and quivering strife,
Therein a portion claim.

This, this is holy;—while I hear
These vespers of another year,
This hymn of thanks and praise,
My spirit seems to mount above
The anxieties of human love,
And earth's precarious days.

But list!—though winter storms be nigh,
Unchecked is that soft harmony:
Their lives who can provide
For all his creatures; and in Him,
Even like the radiant seraphim,
These choristers confide.

FROM THE ITALIAN OF
MICHAEL ANGELO

Yes! hope may with my strong desire keep
    pace,
And I be undeluded, unbetrayed;
For if of our affections none find grace
In sight of Heaven, then, wherefore hath God
    made
The world which we inhabit! Better plea
Love cannot have, than that in loving thee
Glory to that eternal peace is paid,
Who such divinity to thee imparts
As hallows and makes pure all gentle hearts.
His hope is treacherous only whose love dies
With beauty, which is varying every hour;
But, in chaste hearts uninfluenced by the power
Of outward change, there blooms a deathless
    flower,
That breathes on earth the air of paradise.

INDEX TO FIRST LINES

155

157